ZAMEEN

by Satinder Kaur Chohan

SAMUEL FRENCH

Copyright © 2021 by Satinder Kaur Chohan
All Rights Reserved

ZAMEEN is fully protected under the copyright laws of the British Commonwealth, including Canada, the United States of America, and all other countries of the Copyright Union. All rights, including professional and amateur stage productions, recitation, lecturing, public reading, motion picture, radio broadcasting, television, online/digital production, and the rights of translation into foreign languages are strictly reserved.

ISBN 978-0-573-13262-9

concordtheatricals.co.uk
concordtheatricals.com

FOR AMATEUR PRODUCTION ENQUIRIES

United Kingdom and World
excluding North America
licensing@concordtheatricals.co.uk
020-7054-7298

Each title is subject to availability from Concord Theatricals, depending upon country of performance.

CAUTION: Professional and amateur producers are hereby warned that ZAMEEN is subject to a licensing fee. The purchase, renting, lending or use of this book does not constitute a license to perform this title(s), which license must be obtained from the appropriate agent prior to any performance. Performance of this title(s) without a license is a violation of copyright law and may subject the producer and/or presenter of such performances to penalties. Both amateurs and professionals considering a production are strongly advised to apply to the appropriate agent before starting rehearsals, advertising, or booking a theatre. A licensing fee must be paid whether the title is presented for charity or gain and whether or not admission is charged.

This work is published by Samuel French, an imprint of Concord Theatricals. Ltd

The Professional Rights in this play are controlled by Berlin Associates, 7 Tyers Gate, London SE1 3HX.

No one shall make any changes in this title for the purpose of production. No part of this book may be reproduced, stored in a retrieval system, scanned, uploaded, or transmitted in any form, by any means, now known or yet to be invented, including mechanical, electronic, digital, photocopying, recording, videotaping, or otherwise, without the prior written permission of the publisher. No one shall share this title, or part of this title, to any social media or file hosting websites.

The moral right of Satinder Kaur Chohan to be identified as author of this work has been asserted in accordance with Section 77 of the Copyright, Designs and Patents Act 1988.

USE OF COPYRIGHTED MUSIC

A licence issued by Concord Theatricals to perform this play does not include permission to use the incidental music specified in this publication. In the United Kingdom: Where the place of performance is already licensed by the PERFORMING RIGHT SOCIETY (PRS) a return of the music used must be made to them. If the place of performance is not so licensed then application should be made to PRS for Music (www.prsformusic.com). A separate and additional licence from PHONOGRAPHIC PERFORMANCE LTD (www. ppluk.com) may be needed whenever commercial recordings are used. Outside the United Kingdom: Please contact the appropriate music licensing authority in your territory for the rights to any incidental music.

USE OF COPYRIGHTED THIRD-PARTY MATERIALS

Licensees are solely responsible for obtaining formal written permission from copyright owners to use copyrighted third-party materials (e.g., artworks, logos) in the performance of this play and are strongly cautioned to do so. If no such permission is obtained by the licensee, then the licensee must use only original materials that the licensee owns and controls. Licensees are solely responsible and liable for clearances of all third-party copyrighted materials, and shall indemnify the copyright owners of the play(s) and their licensing agent, Concord Theatricals Ltd., against any costs, expenses, losses and liabilities arising from the use of such copyrighted third-party materials by licensees.

IMPORTANT BILLING AND CREDIT REQUIREMENTS

If you have obtained performance rights to this title, please refer to your licensing agreement for important billing and credit requirements.

ZAMEEN was first produced by Kali Theatre at Contact Theatre, Manchester in April 2008. The performance was directed by Janet Steel, Assistant Director Natalie Ibu, Designer Emma Wee, Lighting Jenny Cane, Composer Sayan Kent, Stage Manager Alex Weller. The cast was as follows:

BABA	Bhasker Patel
CHANDNI	Goldy Notay
DHANI	Gurpreet Singh
LAL	Ravin J. Ganatra
SURAJ	Amarjit Bassan

CHARACTERS

BABA – a farmer in his late 50s/early 60s
CHANDNI – Baba's daughter in her mid-20s
DHANI – Baba's son in his mid-20s
LAL – a village moneylender/local commission agent in his 50s
SURAJ – Lal's son in his mid-20s

AUTHOR'S NOTE

With chants of "Kisaan Ekta Zindabad" ("Long Live Farmer-Labourer Unity!"), hundreds of thousands of Indian farmers began a wave of protests against three agricultural reform laws in late 2020, introduced by the government under cover of Covid. One of the world's biggest ever protests, farmers demanded the repeal of laws they believe will fully corporatise Indian agriculture, decimate its small farmers and escalate already alarming farmer suicide rates.

Under the rallying cry of "Delhi Chalo" ("On To Delhi"), the farmers marched on the nation's capital and set up bustling camp cities on its borders, thousands of women among them. Alongside clinics, ambulances, libraries and gyms, Sikh "langar" community kitchens fed both protestors and even the police who tear-gassed, beat and detained them. The Sikh notion of "seva" (service) underpinned the collective spirit. While this is a pan-Indian protest, farmers from the "breadbasket of India" – the predominantly Sikh region of Punjab – are leading the movement.

The agrarian struggles of farmers and their families have been silently simmering for decades. In 2004, I was working as a documentary researcher in Punjab – the land of my ancestors – when I first heard about an "economics of genocide". Since the 1990s, this has led to thousands of farmers committing suicide in killing fields across India from Maharashtra, Andhra Pradesh to Madhya Pradesh, Karnataka and Punjab. According to official statistics, an average of 10,000 farmers, mostly male, commit suicide every year. Unofficial figures are believed to be much higher. Growing up in a largely Punjabi Sikh community in Southall, West London, I held onto romantic images of the golden and verdant lush fields of Punjab and always felt closely connected to my ancestral homeland. On that trip back after a decade away, I was shocked to find out about the ecological devastation of increased corporate/chemical and GM (genetically modified) farming and its tragic impact on small farmers caught in spiralling poverty and debt traps.

Returning to the UK, I felt compelled to write the story of a Punjabi GM cotton farmer and his family. I wanted to capture the convulsive passing of an old India and the dawning of a new globalised one – yet also reflect a global struggle connecting small farmers from Asia and Africa to South America. With no theatre or creative writing experience, that story became my first play – *Zameen*.

Thanks to Arts Council funding, I spent a couple of months living with and interviewing farmers and their families in Malwa, Punjab. In May 2007, I arrived for the cotton-sowing season. In October 2007, I returned for the cotton harvest. I travelled across the cotton belt, visiting dusty, time-warped villages in the southern districts of Bathinda, Moga and Sangrur. As the last of the camels ploughed, the last of the charkhas spun and the last of the handlooms were woven, the outside was already pushing in – via mobile phones, satellite TV, Western snacks, Chinese food and "phoren" dreams.

I stayed with cotton-farming families and immersed myself in the rhythms and routines of village life. I spoke to many beleaguered farmers and their families, to "suicide farmer" families, to moneylenders and young men escaping the depleted land through drink and drugs. I spoke to young women bound by traditional expectations and costly dowries in a society where preference for sons means that female foeticide and infanticide rates are shockingly high. I learnt about GM and Bt cotton crops, plummeting groundwater levels, chemically poisoned soil and water, soaring cancer rates and disrupted seasons. I saw how the Green Revolution, Western-conceived in the 1960s and initially prosperous, had helped push Punjab to the brink of an economic, environmental and climate catastrophe.

It was a heart-wrenching trip, finding out about land and lives in violent transition. Yet it was also a shaping creative journey, in which characters and stories I originally imagined at my desk in Southall came to life through the inspiring, stalwart people I met. I returned with hundreds of photographs and sixty-plus interviews, trying to listen to the Punjabi closely, translating words or phrases that sang with images and metaphors. *Zameen* is written in a heightened folk style, attempting to capture some of the colour and vibrancy of a rural Punjabi language – and the resilient spirit of its people.

Punjab is shaped by a long history of oppression, resistance and fighting injustice. From the Ten Sikh Gurus to revolutionary freedom fighters, Punjabis fought the Mughals and colonial British, suffered Partition and state-sponsored violence during the 1984 genocide and its aftermath. Defined by 'khet, kheti and pind' ('farm, farming and village'), it seems apt that Punjabi Sikhs are driving a protest movement that pits the small farmer against a neo-liberal government and big corporations. It is a lop-sided conflict, which sums up our times. Over a decade before the farmers decided en masse to bravely fight back, together, *Zameen* sought to dramatise the struggles of their changing world.

Thanks to Kali Theatre Company, the play embarked on a UK tour in 2008, long before the wider world caught up with this grave and vital story. The farmers' growing rural plight is finally being highlighted globally, not only through international media but also far-flung Punjabi Sikh diasporic communities and social media savvy younger generations. The original play is followed by a newly added epilogue, bringing *Zameen* into this seismic protest moment.

Ultimately, *Zameen* seeks to capture an insular world, at the very moment when the winds of corporate globalisation and climate change are sweeping in. Its rural characters and themes might seem far away but they are much closer than many in the West might think. From the food we eat, to the clothes we wear, to the lifestyle and consumer choices we make and the values we choose to live by, their fate and destinies are inextricably tied to our own. Through colonialism and neoliberalism, the needs and ways of the West have impacted, often devastatingly, on the rural lives of others. But their rural lives echo in ours too. All over the world, these farmers – effectively global key workers and our environmental guardians – are paying a dangerously high price for change. It remains crucial for all our futures and our shared planet that we listen closely to what they say.

Scene One

(A small village in the cotton rich region of Bathinda, Punjab [formerly "Land of the Five Rivers"], India. Late monsoon season.)

(Beneath sunset skies, the River Ghaggar billows through cotton fields, like a stretch of fiery saffron cloth. The setting sun ignites the crops, which burst with flowers and bristle with new life.)

(A room in a Punjabi pukka (brick and cement) house, painted a vibrant but paint-peeling shade of green. Doors, left and right, lead to the courtyard outside. A manja (charpoy) lies to the left and a peti (tin bridal trunk), sits to the right, draped in a hand-embroidered floral fabric. A jharu (small handheld broom) leans against the peti. A triptych of images hangs on the back wall: a garlanded photograph of a chunni-clad older Sikh woman and portraits of a Sikh Guru and Punjabi revolutionary Bhagat Singh. Traditional stools, a small plastic table and chairs are scattered in the foreground. A steel jug of water and tumbler sit on the table, while a pakhi (handheld fan) and Punjabi newspaper have been flung aside on a stool. Discarded tin containers labelled "Bull Dose" in red, white and blue lettering, dot the dusty floor. Through a window, the family cotton field and a solitary Neem Tree are seen on the horizon, bathed in an orange glow.

> *Beyond the house and courtyard, cotton fields unfurl into the distance. As crickets chirrup, laughter from outside, spills into the room.)*

BABA. *(Singing loudly offstage.)*
BRUUUUHAAAA! BRUUUUHAAAA!

> *(BABA dances his way in, followed by CHANDNI. Singing a Punjabi song ["**PUTT JATTAN DE**"]*, BABA performs slow motion bhangra poses, palm on one ear. He wears an orange turban, traditional kurtha top, pyjama and chappals. In a brightly coloured shalwar kameez and sparkling chunni, juttis (traditional shoes) and gold accessories (earrings, necklace and a few bangles), CHANDNI carries a wedding box of jalebis. Both BABA and CHANDNI wear a steel kara (Sikh bangle) on their wrists.)*

CHANDNI. Oh Baba, you haven't danced or sung like that in years...

BABA. *(Continues humming.)*
BBRUUUUHAAAA!

CHANDNI. And did I see you sneak a glassy or three at the wedding?

BABA. A devout Sikh like me? Your eyes deceive you bheti. Ho!
BRUUUUHAAAA!

> *(Despite her hand-waving protestations, a singing and dancing BABA pulls CHANDNI in to dance. CHANDNI giddha dances around BABA, clapping hands to the earth and sky, before collapsing, laughing, onto a stool. She tries pulling BABA down onto another stool.)*

CHANDNI. Sit! Or you'll wilt in this heat!

---
* Licensees are to use the version of Putt Jattan De in the public domain.

BABA. A song to lift us Jat farmers up, out of the soil... BRUUUUHAAAA!

(Knees buckle.) Aaa-hai, ho-ho, my knees ...

> (**BABA** *drops onto a stool, kicking off his chappals and wiping his brow.*)
>
> *(Breathless.)*

... and ... cracked feet – so sore ...

> *(Laughing,* **CHANDNI** *sits before* **BABA** *to knead his knees and feet, as he continues humming the song.)*

CHANDNI. It's not really a song for *all* us Jats, is it Baba?

BABA. Hain? It's our Jat national anthem. When we hear that song, our fiery blood rises, our warrior hearts swell with pride *(Slaps his chest.)* – we all have a duty to dance!

CHANDNI. *(Stops kneading.)* But why always the sons?

BABA. *(Gestures to* **CHANDNI** *to keep kneading.)* It's about us all. Sons *and* daughters.

CHANDNI. "Sons of Jats dying for their country. Sons of Jats taking revenge. Sons of Jats holding the arm of Heer..." Always praising the sons, erasing the daughters.

BABA. We know our daughters are the perfect sons our own sons can't be. We don't need to sing about it.

> (**CHANDNI** *kneads* **BABA**'s *knee a little harder.*)

Hai!

CHANDNI. *(Grinning.)* Sorry Baba.

BABA. Well, "perfect" sons, apart from Preeto Kaur. See her leaving her father's house? Scurrying to her new husband's home? Her mother was still wiping tears on the trails of her daughter's wedding dress. When you leave, you better shed a few tears – even if they're not real.

CHANDNI. My tears will run a thousand rivers deep.

BABA. *(Blessing* **CHANDNI***'s head.)* Shaavash. You're more than a perfect son Chandni. You're a Lioness of Punjab too.

CHANDNI. *(Rising.)* Does that mean that one day, I'll roar over my own patch of land?

BABA. It means that now Preeto's married, I must find a husband for you.

> (**BABA** *stretches his legs.* **CHANDNI** *distracts herself with the garlanded photo.)*

CHANDNI. These marigolds have faded so quickly. I only hung them up yester— *(Notices something on the garland.)* Ugh! What… is… –?

> (**CHANDNI** *removes the garland and hurls it outside the door.)*

We all so busy we can't throw out a rotting garland?

BABA. Bheti, it's all anyone wanted to talk to me about at the wedding…

> (**CHANDNI** *grabs the jharu and sweeps the floor.)*

CHANDNI. What do you want with roti? Dal or saag –?

BABA. We should start looking soon –

CHANDNI. …or sabji or –?

BABA. Bheti…?

CHANDNI. *(Throwing down the jharu.)* They wouldn't leave me alone either! Nothing better to do with their time than meddle.

BABA. What will the villagers say if we don't?

CHANDNI. Who cares what they say?

BABA. I have to.

CHANDNI. Should busy themselves marrying off their own children.

BABA. While I busy myself marrying off my own.

CHANDNI. She's barely been gone.

BABA. She would have wanted this.

CHANDNI. I'd rather look after the children at the school – than mother a husband *and* his family.

BABA. Lal once mentioned a travel agent in Jalandhar – who helps smuggle our boys abroad. He could get Dhani there…

CHANDNI. Achaa? So Dhani goes abroad – and I live my life with a fat travel agent from Jalandhar? Looking after your Lioness of Punjab so well.

BABA. Oh Rabba, take a look…

CHANDNI. I don't want to follow up Lal's recommendations. Besides, you saw Preeto's dowry, all laid out on the veranda, like a sacred offering to her husband and in-laws. New television, new cellphones, new cupboard, new cooler, new sofa set, new dish set, new fridge, king-sized bed, queen-sized trunk, money and clothes – snaked in gold chains –

BABA. You forgot the shiny new motorcycle. *(Drifts into a reverie.)* Ho, to roar across the plains of Punjab, tearing through dust storms, hot winds –

CHANDNI. A motorcycle, without which Dhanwant's family threatened to cancel the wedding. Weddings don't celebrate husband and wife. They celebrate the wife's father's wallet. How will you pay for it all?

BABA. *(Angrily.)* That's not your concern bheti! *(Pause.)* Gal sun, my livelihood grows from the fragile stems of a single cotton crop. A simple thread ties me to the land – with the power to strangle me too. I've barely been breathing these past few years. But this year will be different. This year, the thread will unravel, run, run, run... Like those rich harvests of old. Soon, I'll be wealthy enough to send Dhani abroad – and throw you a lavish wedding at the best marriage palace on the GT Road!

> (**CHANDNI** *ignores* **BABA**, *continuing to sweep the floor.*)

I spoke to Dhanwant earlier. He's started working for an Amrikan company investing in Punjab. They're looking into the cotton market here. Could even contract farm our cotton – at a competitive rate too.

CHANDNI. Oh. But isn't his company building the new pipeline?

BABA. They branch into all sorts these days. Chardi kala, Punjab is ripe for picking! Very soon *(Helps up* **CHANDNI**, *tying her chunni into a cotton sack.)*, you'll be slinging a chunni sack on your back to cotton pick *our* riches.

> (**BABA** *admires* **CHANDNI** *in her cotton garb.*)

CHANDNI. The crop does look very full. Like one of her soft embroidered sheets, stretched in the sun, bursting with flowers. Is it the seeds?

BABA. I bought wisely this year, didn't I? We'll shift cotton by the bale load! I'll even put aside cotton for you, to fill pillows and quilts for your dowry trunk.

> (**CHANDNI** *unties her cotton sack, throwing her chunni back around her neck.*)

Then, straight after we harvest this crop, we'll comb the land quickly, sow a bumper wheat crop in time for Vaisakhi. By then, I'll have found you a fine Jat boy.

CHANDNI. *(Sitting.)* You won't need to look too long or too far.

BABA. You've someone in mind already? ... Hain?

> (**CHANDNI** *removes her gold jewellery, laying it on the table.*)

CHANDNI. There's hardly a lack of suitors in these villages. At the wedding, aunts, mothers, matchmakers jostled to speak to me about this boy, that boy –

BABA. There was a demand. We could even compete with that rich girl – o-ho, what's her name? Dhanwant's boss' daughter...?

CHANDNI. Chhaya?

BABA. Haah, Chhaya.

CHANDNI. Her family could buy up all the single men round here if they wanted. There are a few. You noticed?

BABA. Ki?

CHANDNI. Our villages teeming with single boys?

BABA. Hain?

CHANDNI. Aren't enough girls for boys. Not enough wives to go round.

BABA. All this think talk is making you mad. How will we marry you off then?

CHANDNI. Baba, the villagers have spent years getting rid of their baby girls. Dumping their tiny skulls, tiny bones, on the roadside, in rivers, on rubbish heaps. Dissolving them in acid. Why? They're tiny kernels of nature. Not big kernels of profit. But only *now* these women are worried? Worried there aren't enough brides for their sons or grandsons?

BABA. It's a terrible sin on us all bheti. But the villagers are desperate. Not wealthy.

CHANDNI. Better a small price to wash out a girl before birth, than pay for her big dowry later?

BABA. The villagers still believe with sons you invest, with daughters you're in debt. It's an expensive business raising a daughter and dowry.

CHANDNI. *(Kneeling at* BABA*'s feet.)* What if I stayed here longer? Worked on the land with you?

BABA. What's this twisted talk?

CHANDNI. Then I wouldn't need to get married. We wouldn't need to raise a dowry.

BABA. Bheti, you can't grow old here. With the joy of seeing you grow into a woman is the pain knowing that one day soon, I must let you go. You don't belong to me. You don't belong here. You belong to your husband and in-laws. Elsewhere.

CHANDNI. *(Standing.)* If I don't belong here, as your daughter, how am I entitled to half your land?

BABA. It's not your birthright.

CHANDNI. It is. By law.

BABA. Law? We don't live by the law, when we live by tradition.

CHANDNI. What if I don't want to be like Preeto or the others, signing my land over to my brother?

BABA. There's barely enough to divide between sons nowadays. If our daughters sharpen their knives too, what's left? A plot to feed the ants?

CHANDNI. There'll be nothing left when he's finished here.

BABA. I know you'll do what is right. If you don't want to, tell me now. I'll sign it all to him while I still can. Your land lies with your husband. This is Dhani's land.

CHANDNI. In my father's house, I own nothing. In my husband's house, I will own nothing. What do I own Baba? What can I call mine?

BABA. That's the way it is.

> *(Turning away from **BABA**, **CHANDNI** sits, fanning herself with the pakhi. **BABA** notices something on the ground. He picks up the object, wraps it in his handkerchief and stuffs the handkerchief into his pocket.)*

I – I'm – I'm going to the fields.

CHANDNI. You're meant to rest this evening.

BABA. There's a problem with the tubewell.

CHANDNI. Can't it wait 'til tomorrow?

BABA. *(Slipping on his chappals.)* We're at the mercy of a monsoon that hasn't come.

CHANDNI. The crops won't be burnt by the sun overnight.

BABA. Water level dropped again this morning. Could be the motor. I should take a quick look *(Walks towards the door.)*.

CHANDNI. *(Getting up.)* I'll come with you –

> *(Steel pots and pans crash and glass breaks in the courtyard outside. Barefoot, in a grubby kurtha and pyjama, **DHANI** tumbles through the door, collapsing by **BABA**.)*

DHANI. Fitteh moo Chandni! Pots, pans should be tidy stacked. Like she always did.

CHANDNI. *(Rushing to **DHANI**.)* You're bleeding. / You reek of liquor too!

BABA. O-ho / get him some water.

(**CHANDNI** *goes to pour a tumbler of water from the jug, slapping* **DHANI** *as she goes.*)

CHANDNI. Bewakoof!

DHANI. Here now. Going to wedding. Going get dressed.

BABA. Kala bhoot. We've been and come back.

(**CHANDNI** *holds out the tumbler.* **BABA** *paces, glancing between* **DHANI** *and the land.*)

CHANDNI. Better you missed it, dear brother.

DHANI. But I want to see chunky Preeto – in her dainty red dress.

(**CHANDNI** *throws the tumbler of water in* **DHANI**'*s face.*)

Teacherwali, there's a drought! Your father could have poisoned his fields with that!

BABA. (*To* **CHANDNI**.) Wipe that up –

(**CHANDNI** *gets a cloth and wipes up the water on the floor.*)

– then clean up his cuts!

(**CHANDNI** *gets another cloth to tend to* **DHANI**'*s wounds.*)

DHANI. (*Holding out his hands.*) Look – my bleeding hands. Blood from my lifeline, trickling across my heart line... my fate line... shall I lick it? See what destiny tastes of? (*Licks his hand.*)

CHANDNI. (*Tries dabbing at* **DHANI**'*s cuts.*) Keep still! ... Wait, there's something on your vest –

DHANI. What is it?

> (**CHANDNI** *plucks a small object off* **DHANI**'s *vest.* **BABA** *readies to leave.*)

Did it crawl out of my peasant heart?

> (**CHANDNI** *throws the small object outside.*)

BABA. *(At the door.)* Put him to sleep.

DHANI. *(Laughing.)* But the riverbeds are dry.

BABA. After you've fed him some roti.

CHANDNI. He's had his fill. Eats away at others, after he's eaten away at himself.

DHANI. *(Holds out his hands.)* Baba? See these hands, pulsating with life? Your peasant hands just carry the weight of bad fate. Blood clogs the lines on your palms. Clogs the furrows in your fields.

> (**BABA** *shoots a look back at* **DHANI** *before leaving.*)

(Shouts after **BABA**.*)* My wounds will heal! Your scars will only dig deeper!

> (**CHANDNI** *throws the cloth at* **DHANI**. **BABA** *crashes into the pots and pans off-stage.*)

BABA. *(Shouts.)* O-ho! Tidy up out here! There's broken glass everywhere!

DHANI. Yes Chandni. Before someone cuts themselves, spills bloody poison everywhere.

CHANDNI. Do I have a choice?

DHANI. *(Laughs.)* No sweet sister. You don't.

> (**CHANDNI** *grabs the jharu. The lights cut out.*)

CHANDNI. *(Shouts.)* Baba, the electricity's gone! Baba?

DHANI. Kaljug has come. The age of darkness has swallowed the light.

> (CHANDNI *pushes* DHANI *out of the way as she rushes into the courtyard.*)

Let the current dam burst open...

> (DHANI *leaps up and moves around the room, searching for rupees.*)

...so I can find rupees rupees rupees...

> (*The light returns but flickers.* DHANI *finds a moneybox buried inside the peti. He stuffs a handful of rupees into his trousers and closes the peti.*)

It's going to be a starry starry night.

> (DHANI *rushes to sit on the manja.* CHANDNI *walks back in with a steel bowl of spinach and a knife.*)

CHANDNI. Badmaash. If you're all cut up inside, do you have to take a knife to your father too?

> (CHANDNI *sits on a stool and hand chops the spinach into the bowl.*)

(Stops chopping.) Shouldn't you help your father now the harvest is near?

DHANI. Mmmmm...nay.

CHANDNI. Baba sweats it in the fields all day. I work at the school, on the land, in the house... What do you do?

DHANI. I ... I ...

CHANDNI. Wake up in the midday sun to drink whisky, ride high on bhang, afeem and poppy husk bhukki!

DHANI. *(Hovers behind* CHANDNI.*)* Catch up sister. I wake up in the midday sun, smear boot polish all over my scalp, before the scorched sun melts its vapours into my humming brain...

> (**DHANI** *flicks over the bowl, which crashes to the ground.* **CHANDNI** *wields the knife.*)

CHANDNI. Every day, a rotting carcass, filled with the stench of death.

DHANI. Sorry, who are you? Because you are not my mother.

CHANDNI. Better she's dead than see her bleeding drunk of a son like this.

> (**DHANI** *seizes* **CHANDNI***'s wrist. They pull the knife between them.*)

DHANI. She'd be happy with you? Even chunky Preeto found a husband. You've gone stale on the marriage market, sprouting cotton white hairs in your father's house.

> (**DHANI** *lets go of the knife, as* **CHANDNI** *pushes him away. She sits, gathers the spilt spinach to resume chopping.* **DHANI** *paces, then drops prostrate on the manja. Pause.*)

Chandni?

> (**DHANI** *gets up and circles* **CHANDNI**.)

Little Bibi?... Little Bibi?...

> (**DHANI** *tries to tickle* **CHANDNI**, *who pushes him away.*)

> (*Sings.*)

LITTLE BIBI!

CHANDNI. Drown and die.

DHANI. Guess what I did today...

(DHANI *grabs a handful of spinach and chews.* CHANDNI *pushes away* DHANI*'s hand.*)

Guess!

(CHANDNI *continues chopping the spinach.* DHANI *picks up an empty "Bull Dose" tin to wear as a hat.*)

Haah, haah, I've been at Dev's drink shack all day, knocking back chemicals. On my way back, Pawan Singh was spraying his crops, flying so golden sparrow high, his feet weren't even touching the ground! When I smelt it cooking in the wind, I had lift-off too! New medicine for his crops, sold to him by... wait for it...

(CHANDNI *stops chopping and glares at him.*)

Wait... Ready? *(Pause.)* Suraj!

(*The tin hat falls.* CHANDNI *resumes chopping.*)

So I went looking for him.

(CHANDNI *ignores him.*)

I've just seen him!

CHANDNI. Achaa? Did you take a nuclear rocket from the village to Amrika? Or did it disintegrate on take-off, along with your boot-polished brain?

DHANI. No, I met him here. In the village.

(CHANDNI *shoots* DHANI *an exasperated look.*)

I did meet him. He's really here.

(CHANDNI *stops chopping.*)

CHANDNI. In the village?

DHANI. Haah.

CHANDNI. But... he's... he's in Amrika...

DHANI. All-Amrikan superheroes can fly back to visit!

CHANDNI. How... how is he?

DHANI. Bigger. Stronger. Wealthier. Fairer-skinned. More handsome. *(Laughs.)* So many tales to tell of Amrika! ... Imagine, if you'd said yes, you'd be telling those tales too.

CHANDNI. Why do you –?

DHANI. Amrika is a long way from secret liaisons by the river, lying in the fields, under a shady tree...

CHANDNI. How could I have abandoned you all back then?

DHANI. "Abandoned"? You could have helped us from there. Suraj got a high-paid job. Earns thousands and thousands of dollars a year. Lives in an Amrikan Maharaja's palace. With a courtyard, size of a cricket pitch. Dozens of rooms, marble floors, stuffed with giant TVs, stereos, computhars. Not one – but two jeeps, he drives like an Amrikan cowboy, pumping the latest bhangra music around New York! You should have married him when you had the chance. Made a difference to all our wretched lives.

> (**BABA** *enters, wiping his forehead with the tail end of his turban. He sits down on a stool, fanning himself with the pakhi.*)

CHANDNI. *(To* BABA.*)* I'm going to put on the saag.

> (**CHANDNI** *exits, carrying the bowl of spinach.*)

DHANI. Baba?

BABA. *(Distracted.)* Hmmm?

DHANI. I've just seen Suraj.

BABA. Suraj?

DHANI. He's back from Amrika.

BABA. Good. Good.

DHANI. *(Drunkenly pacing.)* Now there's a man who enjoys his Amrikan money. Not like his paise-pinching father Lal. Took me to Mohan's roadside shack for a few drinks, downed with a slap-up roti. Gave me fine advice about Amrika. Bought me a whisky bottle from there too – but it soiled my shirt when it smashed outside… *(Rubs his kurtha top.)*

BABA. The noble land flows through your veins – but you'd rather be the full-time village drunk?

DHANI. I love what I do! You know how much time and effort it takes to be the village drunk? Wallowing in my own liquor pool of shame? Really quite an honour if you think about it.

BABA. Honour? When you've heaped nothing but shame upon this family?

DHANI. I lost my honour a long time ago Baba – and I'm not saving yours.

BABA. Your age, I was already out there. Working the land by my grandfather's, my father's side. Once, fathers and sons clattered, clunked tools. Now, even the rake striking the ground is deafening. When I look around, I see no one. Only empty land, almost like desert, stretching for miles…

DHANI. You think I was made for peasant life? Look at these hands *(Holds up his hands.)*. Built for a better life far from here. Even doused in blood, they've got distant lands written all over them.

> (**DHANI** *stumbles around the room and picks up the newspaper.*)

Read the paper! Read about the ones who made it when they got away. Hain – you can't! You can only read the lines in the water, the soil, clouds, sky. But even those lines have become crooked – and aren't telling you the truth anymore.

(**DHANI** *throws the newspaper at* **BABA**'s *feet.*)

BABA. I don't need to read to know about the ones who never make it. Sons cheated of their money. Sons trapped in foreign prisons, left there to die.

DHANI. Same as here then. But better a prison out there, than the fortress walls round here. *(Staring out towards the land. Pause.)* Why can't you just sell an acre?

BABA. So you can build your father's funeral pyre, out of cotton sticks?

DHANI. I wouldn't fill the air with their pollution.

BABA. Did she give birth to you to tug my beard in humiliation every day?

DHANI. She saved the seeds after every harvest. Dropped them in big earthen pots for you to sow again the season after. Seeds passed from your great-grandparents to you – in one… seamless… cycle. It's not like that anymore is it? The old cycles are broken. Dead. Those sterile new seeds you buy – can't be saved for the next life. Because they only have one life. No connection to the past. No connection to the future. Glug chemicals to grow and survive, before they flower and die. Seeds aren't seeds. Sons aren't sons. An acre isn't just an acre.

BABA. I can't take the risk.

DHANI. But you know all about risks! Gambling on monsoons, markets, with borrowed money, on borrowed time. Gambling with seeds those big people tell you to buy. *(Pause.)* Actually, no, you're not a gambler. You're a magician. Baba, how are the crops? Performing any illusions lately? Any Indian cotton rope tricks?

BABA. *(Jumps from his stool.)* I'll make you a man right now if I have to!

> (**BABA** *charges at* **DHANI** *and pins him against a wall.* **CHANDNI** *rushes in, trying to pull them apart.*)

CHANDNI. Baba stop! You're hurting him! Stop!

> (**LAL** *enters, wearing a too tight Western jacket and trouser suit.* **BABA** *moves away as* **DHANI** *slides to the floor.* **CHANDNI** *tends to* **DHANI**.)

LAL. Oh balle balle…

BABA. *(To* **CHANDNI**, *pointing at* **DHANI**.*)* Get him out of here.

> (**CHANDNI** *tries to drag* **DHANI** *towards the door.*)

DHANI. Lalji? My kidneys for a ticket to Amrika?

CHANDNI. Chup kaar!

DHANI. Two for the price of one?

LAL. *(Waving away* **DHANI**'s *liquor breath.)* If I were in the kidney business, which I'm not, I'd want top quality kidneys – not ones pickled in alcohol. Chandni, looking elegant as always.

> (**CHANDNI** *forces a smile at* **LAL**, *as she pulls* **DHANI** *into the courtyard.* **BABA** *calms himself, places a stool in front of* **LAL** *and sits on another stool.* **LAL** *takes a jalebi from the box. He gobbles the jalebi, licking his fingers clean.*)

Delicious. *(Turns to* **BABA**.*)* You've been looking for me?

BABA. Haah, haah, I –

LAL. By the way, you heard the news?

BABA. Terrible news. They found Lokraj –

LAL. News about my son? My youngest just returned from the Great States of Amrika – and bought me this brand new suit! I could have done with a size larger. But how was my boy to know while he's been piling up the dollars, his dear old father's been piling on the pounds?

>   (**LAL** *pats his stomach and chuckles.*)

BABA. I heard Suraj was back.

LAL. Back from his luxury mansion, his top dollar job in New York. He bought me this too! *(Takes out a top of the range cellphone.)* So I can keep in touch with him wherever his big business takes him in the world. Cellphone, camera – computer too. Here, let's take a photo of you! *(Holds up the phone to take a photo of* **BABA**.*).*

BABA. Nay, nay Lal, I don't –

LAL. *(Thrusting the phone in* **BABA**'s *face.)* Say "Pakora!"

BABA. Pa-kora...

>   (**LAL** *takes a photo and looks at it on his phone.*)

LAL. Handsome! Smoothes out the furrowed brow, sunburnt crevices on your face. *(Shows* **BABA** *the photo.)* One second Baba's here. *(Deletes the photo.)* The next, Baba's gone. Such blessed sons I have. You couldn't even get it right with one.

BABA. Fate hasn't deemed it that way.

LAL. *(Putting the phone away.)* Fate is just a convenient excuse for people who should try harder.

BABA. I pray he'll still change his ways.

LAL. *(Sitting in a plastic chair.)* What can I do for you?

BABA. Lalji, the crop is guzzling fertiliser, chemicals, water, as if it's a five hundred foot banyan tree –

LAL. You did as I told you? Like it says on the packets? On the tins?

BABA. Exactly as you told me.

LAL. Those miracle seeds are designed to grow into a super strong crop. Need to guzzle to grow.

BABA. Rice crops guzzle water. Eucalyptus trees guzzle water. Not cotton crops. I can't afford to keep spending rupees I don't have.

LAL. I never said it would be cheap.

BABA. You didn't say it would be this expensive either.

LAL. Baba, you're a farmer standing on the frontline between Nature and Science. You've planted seeds created in the best science labs in the world. Miracle seeds, with special genes, designed to control the forces, fluctuations of nature. Designed to fight sun, wind, rain. Fight pests, starvation, disease. Make fields flourish. The whole world looks to clever farmers like you to sow the seeds of profit and progress – seeds created from a science that has flown men to the moon! *(Pause.)* Remember when the youthful Baba Singh reaped the rewards of the Green Revolution?

BABA. *(Looks towards the fields.)* Prosperous times... when our grain became plenty. When Punjab fed the famished stomach of India. We used machines to speed up produce, sprinkled new seeds, new chemicals as if magic dust –

LAL. If we hadn't revolutionised your ways, you wouldn't have sat on the big crops, big rupees that came with it.

BABA. I took a few clever risks. Profited a great deal too. *(Pause.)* But the land lost something. I lost something. That glorious revolution faded. A mere memory, stitched by a few straggly threads.

LAL. What is this talk? The Green Revolution created the Great Baba Singh!

BABA. We stopped our Bharat Mata, our India, from holding out a begging bowl to the world – not realising the begging bowl passed to us.

LAL. ... And the new Gene Revolution will remake you. Those straggly threads will swell into bales and bales of cotton. White gold Baba Singh!

BABA. Lalji... I need another loan.

LAL. Paid off your last few?

BABA. It's expense after expense. I can't run the world on a few rupees.

LAL. My pockets aren't as deep as the three hundred foot tubewells you farmers enjoy digging.

BABA. I'm selling the milk of my only buffalo, depend on my daughter for a few meagre rupees. Pity a father trying to fend for his family.

LAL. What about this father? Who will feed my family, while I prop up all the village farmers.

BABA. I've told you I'll pay back every rupee I've borrowed. But I can only start repaying the debt once I have a crop to sell. Last year was a bad year trying out the new seeds – the year before that, the terrible drought, the year before that the monsoon –

LAL. A bad few years. Still here we are. Waiting.

BABA. We're only a few days away. *(Joins his hands together.)* I've worked hard. Invested all I have – and don't have...

LAL. I just want a repayment...

BABA. I need a little more time...

LAL. ...or... I can take a little land. Zameen.

BABA. What?

LAL. Zameen. I can take a little land as repayment. While I wait.

BABA. My land? But I need all my land to settle the debt.

LAL. A little land won't make a difference.

BABA. *(Angrily.)* I'm a Jat farmer. Son of the soil. Generations strong. Take my land away – I swear I'll take your life away –

LAL. *You're* threatening *me*?

BABA. *(Grabs* **LAL.***)* I'll chop you up small piece by small piece. Then burn down your house – so those paper rupees you covet, will mix with your bones and ashes, to make a rich paste that I'll smear all over my stolen land!

LAL. OK, OK , Baba Singh, careful with my suit!

BABA. Not so long ago my forefathers gave your forefathers work on our land, when nobody – nobody – in this village would breathe their polluted air. As a child, you begged me for food. Now you talk to me this way? My land? Untouchable, you wouldn't dare.

LAL. "Untouchable"? Is that so? That's why the past is firmly in the past and here we are, hierarchy toppled in the present. Now, my wealth makes me untouchable for the likes of you. Moneylenders out there would have swallowed you, your family, your land, in one ravenous gulp by now. Moneylenders who will still refuse you more loans – plus the banks that blacklisted you a while ago.

> *(***LAL*** moves to leave.* ***BABA*** *wipes his face with the tail of his turban, hurrying after him.)*

BABA. Lalji, please, let's be reasonable.

LAL. I didn't work myself up from the dirt, spread manure for your crops, skin and clean out the flesh of your dead cattle, for you to hurl me back there. I've lived on the side of the shadows where the sun sets. Heard steel dishes I accidentally touched, crash into water, into fire. At school, I was the first in my family to wield a stick of chalk, yet they sat me apart from the others. At the gurdwara, they didn't let me pray to a God I believed moulded us all from the same clay. They'd make me wait there, 'til the others finished their holy meal, before I could eat my polluted one. After my mother died, we had to carry her to the outskirts, where scavengers circle, burning her away from the untainted souls of your ancestors. *(Pause.)* But when I learnt how to handle death with my own hands, scraped out its insides, threw its carcass to the dogs and vultures, hung its skin out to dry, I didn't feel cursed. I felt alive. *(Pause.)* I've fought for every scrap of food, every piece of knowledge, every blessing, every rupee that has come my way. I threw off those leather shackles you village people bound me in. I won't be bound by them again.

BABA. Forgive me. I – I shouldn't have spoken to you that way.

> *(Long pause. **LAL** walks by the table, spotting the gold jewellery.)*

LAL. How much do you need?

BABA. A small loan. Three thousand rupees?

LAL. *(Takes out his wallet.)* As you know, there'll be fifty five per cent interest.

BABA. Fifty five per cent?

> *(**LAL** starts to put his wallet away.)*

Fine.

> *(As **LAL** takes out wads of cash, his phone rings with an American Star-Spangled Banner ringtone.)*

What's that noise?

LAL. *(Smiling.)* The future. *(Answering his phone.)* Hallllllo. *(Pointing to the phone.)* My son!... Hain? Haah. Haah... Nay nay, don't do that... Increase, not decrease... Stand firm... Trust me... *(Pause.)* Just three more houses to go... *(Smiling.)* Then we'll fight over buttery rotis like old times! ... Back soon puth. *(Hangs up and puts away the phone.)* Now, three thousand rupees... *(Counts the money and hands it to* **BABA***.)* My crop as much as yours.

BABA. I also need...

LAL. Haah?

BABA. ...more "Bull Dose".

LAL. More of the same? Or can I interest you in The Company's "New, Improved" chemical warfare version? Baba, the world is constantly developing, forever evolving. Wonder of Science. "New, Improved Bull Dose" blows the snakes and weeds right out of the rice water – and er, the cotton crops. Imported from abroad – exclusive sale only in Punjab.

BABA. Whatever you recommend.

LAL. Naturally, the best brand costs a few more rupees.

> *(***LAL*** takes out an inkpad, a notebook bound with red ribbon and a blank piece of paper.)*

Banks open from ten to five. Moneylenders open twenty four hours. For a small fee, I'll throw in delivery too.

> *(***LAL*** unties the ribbon. He places the blank piece of paper inside the notebook and scribbles inside the notebook.)*

Thumbprint here –

> *(***BABA*** signs his thumbprint in the notebook.* ***LAL*** *turns to the blank page.)*

And... here.

    (**LAL** *presses* **BABA**'s *thumb on the inkpad and then, onto the blank paper.*)

BABA. Careful Lalji.

LAL. *(Holds* **BABA**'s *thumb aloft.)* They say the moneylender and farmer are like nail to flesh. I've been fair to you Baba. Not even a sale deed, in case you can't pay, when we should have one.

    (**LAL** *blows the thumbprint dry. He puts the inkpad and notebook away.*)

BABA. I'll start repayments as soon as the harvest is in.

LAL. Once, I was destined to be the hired help on your land. Now, here I am lending loan after loan to the Great Baba Singh. How the mighty Jats have fallen.

BABA. Life is a charkha spinning wheel. Sometimes you spin the wheel. Sometimes the wheel spins you.

LAL. These days, that wheel is spinning faster than it's ever spun. Be careful. Or it might crush you underfoot.

    (**LAL** *begins walking out, pretending to notice the jewellery for the first time. He picks it up.*)

BABA. *(Proudly.)* Chandni's, from her mother. *Her* mother's before her. Carried on foot, all the way from Pakistan, during the Great Divide –

LAL. *(Twirling the jewellery.)* Needs a sophisticated woman to wear it well…

    (**BABA** *looks confused.*)

My wife.

BABA. *(Folds his hands together.)* No. No.

    (**LAL** *clasps the jewellery shut in his hands.*)

(Lunges for the jewellery.) You can't!

LAL. Another loan?

BABA. *(Throws the rupees at* **LAL.***)* Take it back! That gold is worth more than your money! That's Chandni's set! From her mother! For her wedding day!

LAL. A sufficient token of repayment...

BABA. *(Hands clasped.)* Lalji, I beg you.

LAL. Like I did? Or we could cancel your new loan, clear your mounting debt. Then I won't need to take this. Just one big repayment made in land, right now.

> *(***BABA** *stays silent.* **LAL** *holds the jewellery in his folded hands.)*

Sat Sri Akal Baba Singh.

> *(***LAL** *exits. Slowly,* **BABA** *stoops to gather the scattered rupees from the floor.)*

Scene Two

(Night. The courtyard. In silvery moonlight, the cotton field forms a hazy outline on the horizon. The silhouette of the Neem Tree looms large. After an electricity blackout, a small oil lamp flickers in a corner. A bundle of dry cotton sticks lie in another corner. A manja, charkha (spinning wheel) and chulha stove are dotted around. A steel plate of food lies untouched on the ground. **BABA** *paces. In a simple shalwar kameez and chunni,* **CHANDNI** *sits on the manja, embroidering a phulkari (traditional Punjabi tapestry).*

CHANDNI. If you find my saag so tasteless, what hope for my husband?

BABA. *(Turns.)* Hmmm?

CHANDNI. *(Pointing.)* Your saag and roti?

BABA. I'm not hungry bheti.

CHANDNI. A spindly Jat farmer if ever I saw one. To plough through the courtyard, you need to be a man of Sikh steel – keep your strength up.

*(***BABA*** sits on the manja.)*

Why don't you sleep?

BABA. *(Getting up.)* I'm not tired.

CHANDNI. *(Stops embroidering.)* What's wrong?

BABA. Bheti, I... I...

CHANDNI. Haah?

BABA. I – I was – thinking about – replacing the motor, for the tubewell. It's spluttering diesel everywhere.

CHANDNI. *(Continues embroidering.)* Should have lasted longer than it did. One of the boys can take a look.

> (**BABA** *nods. Pause.*)

BABA. *(Looking around.)* The world seems quieter here than it used to.

CHANDNI. Now your beloved son is finally asleep.

BABA. As if all the noise has been sucked out of the village... spilled far away.

> **CHANDNI** *(Sings the Punjabi folk song* [**"CHARKHA MERA RANGLA"**].*)*

BABA. *(Smiling.)* Echoes still dance around.

CHANDNI. Trinjan. When the women ruled the courtyard with their charkhas and manjas. Spinning cotton and gossip 'til the stars spun into sleep.

BABA. You were such a good spinner. Always winning the competitions.

CHANDNI. The best. She taught me well. *(Runs to the charkha.)* The older women sat here – singing of fights, separations. The younger ones sat there *(Points.)*, singing of longings, laughter yet to be had, with husbands yet to be met and married.

BABA. *(Laughing.)* You women. You were so loud. Louder still with your giddha dances... The music of the charkhas would whir round the yard. Then stop *(Claps.)* The air trembling, the ground shaking beneath an army of stamping feet *(Stamps.)*.

CHANDNI. Then all the girls married. Left. *(Pause.)* I'm still singing. But I don't remember the words so well anymore.

---

* Licensees are to use the version of Charkha Mera Rangla in the public domain

BABA. Don't worry bheti. Just get ready to spin the yarn of a bountiful harvest.

CHANDNI. *(Tips the charkha.)* The charkha spins. The world spins. Our lives spin. Round and round and...

(Pause.)

BABA. Bheti... Lokraj passed away today.

CHANDNI. Uncle Lokraj?

BABA. Bhopal Singh told me, on the way to the fields.

CHANDNI. Oh Rabba, what happened?

BABA. He went to cut down some fodder in the morning. They carried him home, dead, in the afternoon. He had drunk pesticides... *(Pause.)* O-ho. Lokraj. Such an honourable man. His great-grandfather led the farmers against the British. Lokraj always tried to sign me up to the Party – to his Red Revolution. He'd say, 'Baba Singh, you can't till the land without tilling its politics'. Those days, we were strong as oxen together, powerful enough to be heard. Today, our bones blacken with toil, we struggle alone, no-one listens. *(Pause.)* Death was standing right over him. Standing over Kulpreet, their girls too.

CHANDNI. What will Auntieji do? Four daughters? No income? *(Pause.)* I got paid yesterday. *(Heads inside.)* It's not much –

BABA. I'll give her tomorrow's milk money...

CHANDNI. She'll need more.

> *(***CHANDNI** *disappears inside.* **BABA** *walks to the edge of the courtyard, looking towards the cotton field.)*

(Returning.) Baba, did you take money from the trunk?

BABA. No bheti.

CHANDNI. I'm sure I put it... *(Pause.)* Besharam! I'll rip off his skin!

>*(CHANDNI rushes back inside.)*

BABA. Bheti!

CHANDNI. *(Offstage.)* Dhani! Dhani!

BABA. O-ho let him sleep! Leave it 'til tomorrow!

CHANDNI. *(Offstage.)* Get up! Get –

>*(CHANDNI rushes back to the courtyard.)*

He's gone.

BABA. Gone?

CHANDNI. He's not there. He's taken the money.

>*(Pause. CHANDNI runs back inside, panicked.)*

BABA. Bheti?

>*(CHANDNI walks back outside, shaking.)*

Bheti?

CHANDNI. He's taken the gold. He's taken it.

>*(BABA holds her tightly.)*

It's all I have of her. All I have.

>*(BABA nods. Long pause.)*

BABA. Bheti, I have –

>*(A voice from the darkness.)*

SURAJ. Hey, in the courtyard! Like old times.

>*(SURAJ enters in a "I Love Amrika" T-shirt, denim jacket, jeans and cowboy boots.*

A cola bottle is stuffed in one pocket and sunglasses, in another. He carries a stack of "New, Improved! Bull Dose" containers. **BABA** *rushes to* **SURAJ**, *as* **CHANDNI** *turns away, using her chunni to dry her eyes.)*

BABA. Aaja putthar. Aaja. Looking so fit, so strong. Kiddha?

SURAJ. Couldn't be better Uncle. Hey Chandni.

CHANDNI. *(Half turns.)* Sat Sri Akal.

BABA. *(Pointing to the containers.)* I've been expecting those.

SURAJ. Yeah, sorry I'm late Uncle. Still on Amrikan time.

BABA. *(Laughs.)* Nay, I'm glad you made it. *(Taking the containers.)* Here, let me... *(Gestures towards the manja.)* Please, sit putthar.

SURAJ. I ...should get back. I'm helping Dad with some business.

BABA. Theek theek. Actually, I've business too... Chandni, I'll be back soon.

CHANDNI. Where you going?

BABA. The fields.

CHANDNI. You just came from there –

BABA. I've got a little work left.

CHANDNI. You've been awake since dawn –

BABA. I'll be wide awake 'til dawn tomorrow if I don't go now.

CHANDNI. Leave the containers. You're tired. They're heavy.

SURAJ. Uncle, it's dark and late. Wait 'til first light.

BABA. Full moon – plenty of light to do a little work.

CHANDNI. *(Readies to go.)* I'll come with you.

BABA. Bas! I'll manage.

> (**BABA** *rushes off, struggling to carry the containers.*)

SURAJ. Wow, looking much older than when I saw him last.

CHANDNI. The land runs right through him. It's worse trying to keep him away.

> (**SURAJ** *slaps a mosquito.* **CHANDNI** *stifles her laughter, as she sits on the manja.*)

SURAJ. Biting, sucking since I arrived.

CHANDNI. *(Laughs.)* You really have been away. Even mosquitoes know blood from outside tastes sweeter.

SURAJ. *(Looking towards the fields.)* Is that the Neem Tree?

CHANDNI. Haah, the blessed Neem. We're still waiting for the fruits to flower this year. It's so late already.

SURAJ. We'd sit under there for hours…

CHANDNI. In the tree's embrace. Honey-scented flowers falling like Himalayan snow on our sun-drenched –

> (**SURAJ** *slaps another mosquito. He walks towards the Neem Tree and takes out the cola bottle. He opens it and cola fizzes everywhere. He takes a quick swig and offers the bottle to* **CHANDNI**, *who waves it away.*)

SURAJ. If your father was a savvy businessman –

CHANDNI. *(Laughs.)* He's a farmer.

SURAJ. …he could make a small fortune selling bits of that tree to cure all the villagers' ills – bark, leaves, fruit, seeds – the whole lot.

CHANDNI. It's the "village pharmacy". Baba calls it the "Free Tree". He'd never charge the village to use it.

SURAJ. *(Shrugs his shoulders.)* Just an idea. *(Turning to* **CHANDNI.***)* You? I hear you're running the village school.

CHANDNI. The village school would need more than me to save it. I'm a private schoolteacher. Haven't taken over just yet. Preeto Kaur runs it – from our schooldays?

SURAJ. Preeto. How could I forget? Built like a juggernaut, always getting in the way. You two were inseparable.

CHANDNI. Not anymore. She got married today.

SURAJ. I heard. Dhanwant seems like a smart guy.

CHANDNI. Another village wedding… for Baba to rediscover his lost youth.

SURAJ. Sorry I missed it… Hey, I'm sorry about Auntie too.

CHANDNI. You left… Then, she left… Death ate her alive.

> (**SURAJ** *sits on the manja beside* **CHANDNI**. *Pause.*)

We met here a lot didn't we? Under a thick blanket of stars –

SURAJ. *(Laughing.)* If anyone came along, I'd leap behind a buffalo or over the wall – splat, face down in cow dung! Nearly got caught a few times.

CHANDNI. *(Laughing.)* Many times. I've still got that scar, falling off the manja *(Pulls up her shalwar leg.)*, landing on Dhani's broken whisky bottle –

SURAJ. Uncle only a few steps away…

> (**SURAJ** *traces a line over the scar.* **CHANDNI** *quickly pulls her shalwar back down.*)

CHANDNI. Were you going to see me? Seems you've caught up with all the other villagers already.

SURAJ. I'm here aren't I?

CHANDNI. Your father sent you.

> (**SURAJ** *brushes a few rogue hairs from* **CHANDNI**'s *face.*)

You never wrote those letters you promised.

SURAJ. Time is a commodity in short supply in the outside world.

CHANDNI. Ah-ha?

SURAJ. There's not enough of it. Amrikans are even drilling below the ground to find more.

CHANDNI. *(Hits him playfully.)* Bakwaas!

SURAJ. Seriously Chandni *(Moves around excitedly.)*, Amrika is a whole new world. One big bazaar – where you can pick, choose, buy who you are – who you want to be. Everything is available. Anything is possible. *(Puts on his sunglasses.)* I'm living the Amrikan dream and never want to wake up.

> (**CHANDNI** *laughs.*)

Looking cool right?

CHANDNI. Looking bewakoof.

SURAJ. The boys told me I looked cool.

CHANDNI. Dhani and his birdbrained friends? A drunk, blurred "cool"? Head to toe in denim. Boots to make you an Indian cowboy. And those? *(Points to his sunglasses.)* New York might be electric bright. But our night sky won't blind you – I promise…

SURAJ. *(Takes off his sunglasses.)* OK, OK. But the T-shirt – bought in New York, 100% Indian cotton.

CHANDNI. Wah ji wah, very good!

(**SURAJ** *sits back down on the manja.*)

You sat here the night before you left. Next day, I imagined you on every plane overhead, hoping you'd see me in the courtyard. *(Pause.)* What happened when you left?

SURAJ. *(Getting up.)* Well, there was first-class service on the plane. Even beds on board – not like these tatty manjas. I slept a sweet barfi sleep. Woke up in time for New York. Got off the plane, walked into a big job, big company. Worked hard. Got a big promotion. Now I have a big office, overlooking the soft curves of Manhattan, hundreds of people working below me. Every day, my driver picks me up in a shiny big black car – the length of five buffaloes –

CHANDNI. That's what happened?

SURAJ. And here I am – basking in Amrikan success!

CHANDNI. Judging by the time it took your father to brag, success took a while.

SURAJ. I made it didn't I?

CHANDNI. You did.

SURAJ. I've also learnt to value my father since I left. If you had more experience of the outside world, you would too.

(**SURAJ** *walks to the edge of the courtyard.* **CHANDNI** *fiddles with the phulkari.*)

CHANDNI. What really happened?

(Long pause.)

SURAJ. Chandni, it took me... seven months... to get to Amrika.

CHANDNI. Seven months? Did you take a donkey cart? Or a camel?

SURAJ. *(Sitting.)* I was abandoned. In Africa. By my agent.

CHANDNI. You had a job lined up in New York? All the right papers?

SURAJ. That's what we had to tell everyone.

CHANDNI. You never told me.

(**SURAJ** *shakes his head.*)

Africa?

SURAJ. I had to go from Bombay to Africa. The agent told me to lie low, wait for the call. It never came. So I went from Kenya to Ethiopia, to Nigeria, back to Kenya, trying to get to New York. Ate, slept in gurdwaras. Stayed with Punjabi brothers who took me in. So many good people. But I was invisible, floating between one world and the next. No idea where I was going, if I'd ever leave...

(**CHANDNI** *notices something on the ground.*)

What is it?

(**CHANDNI** *shakes her head and flicks something away towards the fields.*)

CHANDNI. Then? ...

SURAJ. Dad found another agent, better connected. He got me on a plane to Amrika. Suraj Singh became Labh Singh – Indian businessman extraordinaire! His identity. My picture in the passport.

CHANDNI. Such good kismet –

SURAJ. Such good counterfeit technology. In New York, I'm renting a small apartment with a few boys. One landed me a job... *(Takes* **CHANDNI**'s *hand.)* Promise not to laugh –

(**CHANDNI** *nods.*)

I spend nights – and days – sewing.

CHANDNI. Ha! *(Snakes the phulkari at* **SURAJ**.*)* Mr. Tailorman, finish this phulkari?

SURAJ. I'm a machine man. In fact, with my sewing machine, I bet I could sew two hundred shirts before you finish that piece.

CHANDNI. You'll make a perfect wife one day!

SURAJ. I get up before dawn, work 'til the early hours. Not that I knows it's night – the bright lights, boarded up windows always feel like day. Then the heat. Oh the heat. Sweatier, steamier than Punjab.

CHANDNI. Isn't it tough there? On your own?

SURAJ. I stay close to the others. Lie low. Some of our boys have disappeared. Others arrested, deported. But fear, hard work is a small price to pay, to belong one day. Anyway, by the time I go back, I'll be legal, so I won't have to worry anymore.

CHANDNI. Legal? How?

SURAJ. Always a way.

CHANDNI. Do you miss it here?

(Pause.)

SURAJ. I want to go back. Get enough money together to buy a gas station in California. I'll hire some of our boys – they'll be cheap, work long hours. I'll take my wife there. We'll raise good Amrikan Desi kids. I'll send money back to Dad, so he can build the biggest kothi in the village – with the biggest courtyard and biggest water tank too! *(Pause.)* Chandni?

CHANDNI. Yes?

SURAJ. Nobody else knows. After all these years, he's just so proud of me...

CHANDNI. We all are. Of course I won't say anything.

> (**SURAJ** *strokes* **CHANDNI**'s *face.* **CHANDNI** *turns her face away.*)

So, what's New York like, Labh Singh?

SURAJ. *(In an American accent.)* Dear Chandni, in New York, there isn't space for sky or time to sleep. It's not a city for a siesta Maharani like you!

CHANDNI. It might be! I've sacrificed my naps for school. *(Pause.)* I miss curling up on a manja, or in our secret spots like we used to. *(Pause.)* Sometimes, as life ebbs away here, I feel like this house, this courtyard are shrinking. The land, the sky seem to be creeping in. *(Pause.)* I often wonder how it would have been if I'd followed you.

SURAJ. *(Laughs.)* No charkhas or chulha stoves for you there!

CHANDNI. I could have got used to it. Like you have.

> (**SURAJ** *is silent.*)

Suraj?

SURAJ. Hmmm?

CHANDNI. You always said you'd wait for me.

SURAJ. People in Amrika don't have time to wait.

CHANDNI. I waited for you.

SURAJ. If you had said yes then, I wouldn't be where I am, looking at you...

CHANDNI. I couldn't leave them.

SURAJ. Could you now?

(Pause.)

Let's walk by the river.

CHANDNI. Suraj, it's late. What if Baba...?

SURAJ. *(Places his finger on* **CHANDNI***'s lips.)* Shhhh. We won't be long – and we won't get caught!

(They giggle. **SURAJ** *winds* **CHANDNI***'s chunni round his hand, pulling her closer. She leads as they run off.)*

Scene Three

> *(Next morning. The courtyard.* **DHANI** *darts around, chasing a gecko. Brandishing a chappal in hand, he stumbles, trips over, flings himself across the manja and crashes into the charkha and chulha stove. He thumps the gecko dead with his chappal, dangles it in the air triumphantly, before placing it delicately in a corner. Then, he collapses in an exhausted heap on the manja, snoring loudly. Shortly after,* **SURAJ** *wanders into the courtyard, a water bottle stuffed in his pocket.)*

SURAJ. *(Calling out.)* Uncle...? Chandni...?

> *(***SURAJ*** *sees* **DHANI** *sleeping. He picks up* **CHANDNI**'s *phulkari, crumpled on the ground, holding it awhile. Folding it, he places it on the manja, before slapping* **DHANI** *awake.)*

Oh Dhani Dhani Dhani! Time to get up yaar! Time to spread the manure! Plough the fields! Water the crops! *(Drizzles water over* **DHANI***.)* Time to get up!

DHANI. *(Shielding his head with his hands.)* Oh stop yaar!

SURAJ. You're not allowed to sleep this late in Amrika, yaar.

DHANI. Says... who?

SURAJ. The Profit Police.

DHANI. No such thing.

SURAJ. If they find you sleeping, not working, the Profit Police will knock loudly at your door – and shake you awake, like this! *(Rolls* **DHANI** *off the manja.)*

DHANI. Ohhhhhhhh stop yaar! I only just got back from last night.

> *(Eyes closed,* **DHANI** *slowly crawls back onto the manja.)*

SURAJ. Next morning now.

DHANI. Tell it to cover up.

SURAJ. *(Sitting.)* Out with the boys again?

DHANI. *(Rubbing his eyes.)* Haah. Headed to Bathinda town. Visited the new Hotel Haveli. Crashed a wedding –

SURAJ. – got kicked out?

DHANI. *(Sits up, slowly recollecting.)* Then found my way back... to the village... spent the evening... chatting... to candidates... for the elections!

SURAJ. Taking an interest in something other than yourself?

DHANI. Who says politicians never do anything for the needy?

SURAJ. A New India *is* dawning.

DHANI. Especially when there's free trade –

SURAJ. Yes!

DHANI. – trading *free* liquor, *free* afeem, *free* bhukki –

SURAJ. Oh yaar –

DHANI. ...for our votes. Now that's a political party to run Punjab – farmer productivity will shoot up! *(Gets up, stretching.)* One candidate asked after you.

SURAJ. Who?

DHANI. Ki patha yaar. Red turbans, blue turbans, yellow, orange, they all talk the same old bak bak, don't they?

SURAJ. Sucha Singh? Dad's friend. He's standing for re-election.

DHANI. Judging by his top-quality bhukki, he's heading for a landslide. We tried calling you from his cellphone, just as I was heading for a headslide...

SURAJ. Phone must have been switched off.

> (**SURAJ** *walks around, feeling the charkha and chulha stove.* **DHANI** *potters.*)

DHANI. Where were you?

SURAJ. Busy yaar.

DHANI. Doing what?

SURAJ. Chasing the past.

DHANI. Not fixing the future?

SURAJ. That too.

DHANI. Who with?

SURAJ. Tell the village loudspeaker?

DHANI. Offended yaar.

SURAJ. You?

DHANI. Should've come with us. Night was rocking. Still is.

SURAJ. This man had commitments.

DHANI. This man has only one commitment. Aaja, let's get a drink!

SURAJ. Busy work day ahead. Cup of chaa would settle me nicely.

DHANI. *(Cranes his neck.)* Chandni doesn't seem to be here.

SURAJ. No? Then you make it.

DHANI. Don't do women's work.

SURAJ. Come on yaar. I've just come from the market. Drove through a horde of farmers, spitting slogans, poking placards, handing out headaches in the road.

DHANI. Should have helped them – and run them over.

(**DHANI** *drops against the manja, as* **SURAJ** *sits.*)

SURAJ. Where is Chandni?

DHANI. *(Shrugging.)* Raising her grey-haired toothless children, fat on pollution, growing old before their time?

SURAJ. When does she finish?

DHANI. When they drop dead. You didn't find out last night?

SURAJ. What?

DHANI. Seen her yet?

SURAJ. Briefly.

DHANI. Ha, I knew it!

SURAJ. I had to drop off supplies here yesterday.

DHANI. That's all you dropped?

SURAJ. *(Play slaps* **DHANI.***)* Yaar, it's been more than two years.

DHANI. Tell me.

SURAJ. *(Smiling.)* She was... as I left her.

DHANI. And?

SURAJ. Nothing to tell.

DHANI. Swear to God.

SURAJ. I swear.

DHANI. Eat a sick cow if you're lying?

SURAJ. I'd beat it, eat it, then jump in the mucky canal! I swear. Anyway, what about *you*?

DHANI. Yaar, I just want to snare a phoren girl – made Punjabi, born Amrikan. They really so tough?

SURAJ. Prickly with attitude! But not when they faint at my feet, thirsting for a taste of real village life. I can only oblige.

> (**DHANI** *bounces around excitedly, before stopping.*)

DHANI. So they're modern girls?

SURAJ. Always teasing, pleasing…

DHANI. *(Jumping up and down.)* Yaar, I can't wait!

SURAJ. 'Til then?

DHANI. In these barren parts?

SURAJ. Hey, even the Amrikan boys agree – "modern girls for single life, village girl for married life". You must have thought about snaring a poor village girl…

DHANI. Poor? If I had to choose, *(Dreamily.)* I'd want a girl like – Chhaya.

SURAJ. Chhaya?

DHANI. She's a rare cotton flower! Petals ready to drop. Marrying Chhaya is more than gaining a wife. Thanks to her big boss father, it's marrying a gold-embossed visa to Amrika too –

SURAJ. – plus a small share in their company affairs.

DHANI. Hadn't thought of that. Still stuck on the high-speed motorcycle and cellphone they'd buy me, identical to yours.

SURAJ. I'd be careful. I hear she's full of thorns.

DHANI. Who cares how sharp? She's offering the finest dowry in all Punjab.

SURAJ. She is?

DHANI. *(Leaping up.)* But I can't hang about waiting for her to call –

> (**DHANI** *runs to the other side of the courtyard, as* **SURAJ** *spins the charkha wheel.* **DHANI** *picks up the dead gecko and dangles it from his fingers.)*

SURAJ. Don't touch that.

DHANI. Thumped it earlier, climbing the ground.

SURAJ. Why?

DHANI. For a gecko high on the early flight! *(Picks up a knife.)*

SURAJ. What are you –?

DHANI. First, I cut off its torso and keep its weaver's thumb of a tail. Chop, chop!

> (**DHANI** *chops off the gecko's torso and flings it towards a ducking* **SURAJ.** **DHANI** *places the gecko tail on a hot plate and gathers cotton sticks to burn under the chulha stove, placing the hot plate on top.)*

As the tail cooks, I pound it to ashes. Before rolling it into a cigarette jet to send me flying full gas to Amrika!

SURAJ. That tail is full of poison.

DHANI. Escape!

SURAJ. *(Readies to leave.)* Not while I'm here.

DHANI. Oh yaar... the gecko's the only reptile with a village voice. Let me silence it for a reason.

SURAJ. I'm serious.

DHANI. *(Picking up the gecko head and torso.)* Look at those eyes – no blinking. Just stuck backwards, stuck forwards. One eye to the past. One eye to the future.

SURAJ. *(Slaps the gecko torso away.)* Isn't it time you did something for the others?

(Pause.)

DHANI. I would have – for her.

SURAJ. Then find a good wife to help in the house, if you can't.

DHANI. Nah. Too much botheration.

SURAJ. We're not chasing frogs or firing slingshots at the elders anymore.

DHANI. When other lands beckon, you can't get stuck in the mire. You've got to bhangra-shake yourself free of those tangled weeds!

SURAJ. I didn't come back for me. I came back to help my father.

DHANI. My father can't even sell an acre of land for me. Your father did everything for you to go.

SURAJ. He knew my life would be one endless time pass if I didn't. I wasn't ready but he kept pushing. Risked all he had. When Chandni didn't –

DHANI. Why doesn't Baba understand? I don't want to stay here to eat the soil. I want to go out there – feast on dollars!

SURAJ. You could do it here – if you really wanted.

DHANI. How dung cake? Through hard work? Honesty? By killing myself for work? Earning nothing, saving nothing, owning nothing? Yet owing everything? At least the old daku bandits were better – robbed the rich, never troubled the poor. These daku governments dress up the rich, after they've stripped down the poor. Nah, too much tension. It's dead here yaar.

SURAJ. Dead because farming's been in the wrong, time-worn hands for too long. Punjab needs new blood, new industry, new money, to make the land pay. It's starting to flow.

DHANI. Ek minute while I choke on my sickle. Flowing where? Through the weeds? Or burnt out fields?

SURAJ. Look at these big companies and mega projects. If you can't make it outside, the outside will come to you. We're all looking out there to make money. But they're looking here to spend less money. What they want and what they buy is what we need to grow and supply as quickly and cheaply as they need it. The government and investors will plough money in. There'll be factories, industrial parks, software hubs – much, much more, right here – on this very land.

DHANI. I don't want a third-class imitation. I want the real thing.

SURAJ. These are big companies. Big projects. They won't be allowed to fail.

DHANI. This is a wasteland. Out there, that's where people grow – in real lands of plenty.

SURAJ. Dhani, it's not as easy to get over there as you think.

DHANI. Don't make me beat my head yaar! I want to be phoren and a crorepati like you. Like Baldev, who's on a number two route to Dubai. Like Kulwant, who's finally made it on a number two to Europe. He walked over mountains, through deserts, forests, took a boat, nearly drowned. Washed up in Italy with other brothers. Got packed in a truck, buried under plastic sheets, between slabs of frozen meat. No room to move, air to breathe, light to see. Tell me, what makes a man go through that if he doesn't think it will change his life? Make him rich and happy?

(*Pause.*)

SURAJ. Outside, the future has already arrived. In these villages, it's spinning in. If you don't keep up, you'll drop off – into nothingness.

DHANI. (*Holds his head.*) O-ho yaar, the only thing that's spinning in – is my head. Why you here so early?

SURAJ. (*Checking his watch.*) I came to see you – and Uncle… is he around?

DHANI. Uncle Sam? He's in –

SURAJ. Your Bapu yaar.

DHANI. He's scratching at the soil. Eating mud for breakfast, lunch, dinner and dreams. Like the rest of the cattle in this dried out trough.

SURAJ. I came to give him a message.

DHANI. Of support?

SURAJ. It's important.

DHANI. He isn't.

SURAJ. Maybe I'll try and find him…

DHANI. I think he's lost.

SURAJ. Will you tell him?

DHANI. He doesn't listen.

SURAJ. Your Amrika could be riding on it…

DHANI. What do you want him to know?

SURAJ. My Dad wants to see Uncle at four.

DHANI. (*Holds up six fingers.*) Four.

SURAJ. Don't let me down yaar.

DHANI. Never. I'll tell him.

> (DHANI *smacks his forehead with his six fingers repeatedly, before stopping.*)

You will help me to get there won't you? Like a brother-in-law?

SURAJ. (*Leaps into a kabaddi position.*) If you're still kabaddi enough!

DHANI. Kabaddi enough? I'm more than WWF enough!

> (*They tussle playfully. With a sleight of hand,* DHANI *picks* SURAJ's *wallet from his pocket without* SURAJ *noticing.*)

Stop, stop! You phoren boys – too tough!

> (*Laughing,* SURAJ *struts around.* DHANI *walks to the chulha stove, waving dollars.*)

Want your wallet? I'll trade it for a ticket out of here!

SURAJ. Lucha lafangha!

> (DHANI *waves the wallet in the air.* SURAJ *tries to grab it.* SURAJ *leaps for the wallet, unaware a pouch has dropped from his pocket, which* DHANI *spots.* DHANI *empties the contents of the wallet on the manja and swipes a dollar note.*)

DHANI. (*Pointing at the wallet.*) Here, take it!

> (DHANI *swoops to the ground to scoop up the dropped pouch, while* SURAJ *gathers up his wallet contents.* DHANI *opens the pouch and takes out a gold jewellery set, stuffing it all back, except for the necklace. He pretends to wear it.*)

Who's this for?

SURAJ. *(Rushing over.)* Give that back!

DHANI. Your secret Amrikan lady? *(Swings his hips and mock kisses the air.)* Or hot village lover? Ohhhh Soniye!

SURAJ. Stop messing around!

DHANI. Such a rich Amrikan! Will you marry me? Slip a green card on my finger?

SURAJ. *(Lunges for the necklace and pouch.)* Dhani!

DHANI. Who's it for?

SURAJ. *(Lunges.)* None of –

DHANI. How much is it worth?

SURAJ. *(Lunges.)* – your business!

DHANI. *(Snatches the necklace and pouch away.)* Why so serious?

SURAJ. Bewakoof idiot!

DHANI. Then I'll just keep it.

SURAJ. Forget me ever helping you out –

DHANI. Oh come on, I'm just playing around – like we used to.

> (**DHANI** *pretends to slip the necklace into the pouch but slips it into his pocket.* **SURAJ** *grabs the pouch and prepares to leave.*)

SURAJ. Make sure Uncle gets the message.

DHANI. Where you going?

SURAJ. I can't sit around here, acting like a village fool, wasting time.

> (**DHANI** *rushes after* **SURAJ** *as he charges off.*)

DHANI. Don't be angry with me yaar.

(**DHANI** *stands alone. He takes out the dollar note and kisses it, before taking out the necklace. He twirls it in the air.*)

Scene Four

(Late afternoon. The cotton field, with the over-arching Neem Tree nearby. Wispy cirrus clouds scratch a crystalline deep blue sky. The slowly setting sun streams rays of fading orange light. Arid reds and browns bleed across the land. Cotton plants droop. Occasionally, a tractor is heard in the distance.)

*(**BABA** enters, wearing a plastic spray tank on his back. He stoops to inspect the crops, before wiping his sweaty brow with a small cloth. He picks up a small rusty tin, swishing with diesel. He picks something off a cotton stalk, squeezes it between his fingers, dropping it into the tin. He moves slowly through the crops.)*

CHANDNI. *(Shouts offstage.)* Baba? *(Pause.)* Ohhhh Baba?

*(**BABA** continues inspecting his crops.)*

(Louder offstage.) Where are you?

*(**CHANDNI** enters, wearing a red shalwar kameez and chunni. She carries a bag of food, stopping when she sees **BABA**.)*

I've been looking for you everywhere. You left without eating again this morning. If you don't eat, how will you work? She was right. With your frazzled brain, skinny frame, you'll fry like a bhatura in the sun.

*(**CHANDNI** takes out paranthas, achaar and a water flask, laying it on the ground.)*

Aaja, eat. I made something special today. *(Pause.)* Baba? What are you doing?

BABA. Rotten little things.

CHANDNI. What is it?

BABA. See how they wriggle.

*(***CHANDNI** *moves closer to inspect the crops.)*

CHANDNI. *(Jumps back.)* They're – they're crawling everywhere! They're, they're – crawling all over the crops!

BABA. *(Holding up a worm.)* Say Sat Sri Akal to the Amrikan Bollworm... King of the Pests... Soldier of the Green and Gene Revolutions!

*(***CHANDNI** *looks across the land, trembling.)*

Look around bheti. There's an entire Green Army on the move. Attacking the length and breadth of our land. Douse these little green soldiers in poison, they just grow another skin – tougher and stronger than the last. Born Amrikan for a reason.

CHANDNI. Oh Rabba. *(Pause. Realising.)* On – on – the garland... in the courtyard... We have to... we have to get rid of them! *(Flaps her chunni at the crops.)*

BABA. *(Grabs* **CHANDNI***'s arms.)* They'll finish what they started.

CHANDNI. *(Flaps again.)* We can pick them off! Or thrash the crops! It's not too late!

BABA. I've picked the worms off, one... by... one, all morning. Squeezed them between my fingers. Dropped them in the tin. Drowned them in diesel. Every time I pick one off, another takes its place. I can't pick them off fast enough. For now, we can only stand by... watch these worms eat the flesh from our crops. Suck the lifeblood from our veins.

(Pause.)

CHANDNI. Why didn't you tell me?

BABA. Worry you?

CHANDNI. Our land is being eaten alive.

BABA. The land is my responsibility.

CHANDNI. *Our* responsibility!

> (**BABA** *shakes his head.*)

Always too proud to ask for help.

BABA. Yesterday, I thought I could save the crop. But today... today... it's all gone...

CHANDNI. When – when did you first see them?

BABA. In the house... I wasn't sure... I came to the fields... Maybe it was my failing eyes... there didn't seem to be many...

CHANDNI. You could have told me then!

BABA. I thought I could get rid of them. Sprayed the crops 'til the chemicals ran out... Suraj brought more... I carried on... the pesticides did nothing but look pretty... just twirled off the crops in the moonlight...

CHANDNI. I should have been helping you.

BABA. When the moon sunk, I felt them sucking moisture out of the air... sucking on the chemicals, feeding, multiplying... Listen! Can you hear that din?

CHANDNI. What is it?

BABA. The worms. Busy about their business. All night, I've watched these green monsters inch their way up the plants, punch tiny half moon holes in the petals, gobble up the flower buds. Watched them burrow their fat little heads into the pods, devour the soft cotton flesh on the inside, their bodies wriggling like fat little dancing girls on the outside. Eating up our five acres of land. *(Pause.)* Bheti, I'm parched.

> (**CHANDNI** *helps* **BABA** *take the tank off his back. She places it on the ground and leads* **BABA** *to sit under the Neem Tree. She helps him drink water from the flask.*)

For months, I've sprinkled, sprayed this parched land with chemicals that have made my skin blister, my eyes burn. *(Runs a handful of soil through his fingers.)* I feel it in the soil. Where this golden land once flourished, now it gasps for air. It's become like desert here – long stretches of barren desert where I can map out my wretched life – see how it all blew away like sand.

> (**CHANDNI** *runs a handful of soil through her fingers.*)

CHANDNI. Remember when I used to smear my face with the soil?

BABA. *(Smiles.)* I do.

CHANDNI. The soil used to be so soft. When she saw me with my muddy face, she'd run after me with a chappal and curses.

> (**BABA** *laughs.*)

She loved this land.

BABA. She knew what the land needed. But I thought I was the clever one who knew best. I've always been a simple man, raised to the rhythms of the land. A language I understood back then. Now, a language I don't understand at all.

> (**CHANDNI** *holds* **BABA.** *He points to the flask and* **CHANDNI** *helps him drink more water.* **DHANI** *stumbles on, brandishing a bottle of whisky.*)

DHANI. Survey the scene! *(Raises the bottle to* **BABA** *and* **CHANDNI.***)* The hard-working farmer and his dutiful daughter. *(Raises the bottle to the fields.)* And mother! Wherever you may be. Good morning to you all!

CHANDNI. *(Gets up.)* It's late afternoon. If ever there was a time Baba needed you here –

DHANI. Sweet sister, as the sun rose, I tried to peel myself into wakefulness. But my body held fast like glue, stuck to the manja with fine whisky dreams of Amrika!

> (**CHANDNI** *strikes the bottle from* **DHANI**'s *hands. The bottle smashes out in the fields.*)

That whisky doesn't come cheap! You'd think we were wealthy zamindars the way you throw that stuff around!

CHANDNI. And I'd think you were a thieving, lizard-eating –

BABA. *(Joining his hands together.)* Bheti.

> (**CHANDNI** *turns away from* **DHANI**.)

DHANI. Where were you last night little sister? Not late for morning registration?

CHANDNI. *(Facing* **DHANI**.*)* Where were you last night rakhri brother? Harvesting our crop?

BABA. *(To* **CHANDNI**.*)* Let him be.

> (**BABA** *rests his head against the Neem Tree, staring out towards the land.*)

CHANDNI. *(Pulling* **DHANI** *aside.)* Our crop has been destroyed by worms –

DHANI. Ahhh, the worms! Haah, I've seen the worms. In moonlit slumbers face down in the soil, they crawl into my ears, my eyes, my belly, all over my skin. Bite into my flesh. Crawl inside my head, eating my dreams. Just like they're eating Baba's fields.

CHANDNI. We've lost the entire crop.

DHANI. At school, my teacher told me cotton was so delicate, it was like "webs of woven wind". White gold. Yet here on my father's land, there's no white gold. Only black death.

> (**CHANDNI** *walks back to* **BABA**, *sitting beside him.* **DHANI** *follows and sits on the other side.* **CHANDNI**, **BABA** *and* **DHANI** *look out into the fields.*)

Where has all the green gone Baba? The trees, bees, butterflies? Fireflies and peacocks? Earthworms? Little birds that chirped as we played out in the fields and you worked the land? Where has all the fruit gone? Where are the lush fields, where there are only limp plants and desert now? Why have the wells once deep with water, all dried up? Wells like the ones where Gulab Kaur, Dhanvir Singh's wife, took her life by drowning. Now, those poor beaten wives just drop to the bottom with a hollow thud *(Claps.)*. The Green Revolution was meant to bring us prosperity. But it drained the colour from our land. Drained the green from our lives. The green and the blood have run from this land, like the sweat from your brow. *(Jumps to his feet and shouts.)* HAIL THE GREEN REVOLUTION! HAIL THE GENE REVOLUTION!... Whatever its name Baba, it's not happening on your patch of land!

CHANDNI. What would you know about revolution? You've been a whisky foot soldier as long as any of us can remember!

DHANI. *(Struts around.)* Time to defect sister. What about the Green Revolution of Amrika? Suraj signed up, armed with his green card and Amrikan dollars. I want to sign up too!

CHANDNI. Sign up? You have to pay up to join. Where will you find the money?

DHANI. Baba, they say dollars grow on trees in Amrika. *(Pulls out the dollar note from his pocket.)* Green dollars. Leafy dollars. Fresh dollars. Dollars that smell of new life. Dollars that feed and nourish you. Make you big, strong and ready to conquer the world! When I reach Amrika, I'll take huge empty bags to collect the dollars *(Throws the dollar into the air.)* as they flutter from the trees. Then, I'll take a ladder, plucking the stubborn ones that refuse to fall. When the bags overflow, I'll come back to the village and just like Suraj, the villagers will hold me aloft – to cheer me like an Amrikan hero. Then Baba, I'll hand you a big bag of money – and the land will come alive again.

BABA. I did what I believed I had to do.

DHANI. Suraj says the whisky is good there too. Jat Daniels they call it. Not like this Desi poison that clouds your mind for days.

CHANDNI. *(Gets up, to* **DHANI.***)* Look around. This isn't about you.

DHANI. It is about me. It's about all of us. How have the other boys left for Amrika, Canada, England, Australia? And I sit here with nothing to do but drink away time?

BABA. *(Rising.)* I also watched my Punjabi brothers leave. Abandon me to live like kings in Western palaces I only dream of seeing. Yes, I believed we'd get wealthy. But I did it for your mother. For Chandni. Dhani, for you.

DHANI. My mother? You should have listened to my mother.

BABA. What can I do now?

DHANI. My mother told you not to risk the little money we had on miracle seeds, fertilisers, pesticides, chemicals that wouldn't cure all our ills… So you sold your livestock. You sold your tractor. You sold my dead mother's valuables. Your daughter's dowry. You sold my dreams of Amrika. In truth, you sold this family down the River Ghaggar for a cotton crop that hangs over our land like a shroud of death. Didn't turn out to be white gold for us, did it Baba?

CHANDNI. Bas! Go! Get away from here! Your tongue is hanging so low, I should nail it to the ground.

DHANI. *(Pushing* **CHANDNI** *aside, to* **BABA.***)* You chose to buy the poison that killed her. Growing it, spraying it all over the land like water going out of fashion. *(Tearing at his kurtha.)* Her bleeding throat. Blisters in her mouth. Boils all over her skin. If you hadn't, she'd still be here, keeping us alive.

BABA. You think her death doesn't torment *me* every waking, working, dreaming hour? I didn't know the water was poisoned. Seeping from the crops. Spreading all over the land. If I had known... When I look at these shrivelled plants, I see them curl up like fingers – and wonder why the land doesn't just pull me under, so I can join her...

> (**BABA** *walks towards the sunset, which emits blood red rays over the arid land. Absent-mindedly, he moves through the crops.* **CHANDNI** *and* **DHANI** *remain within earshot of* **BABA**. *Long pause.*)

CHANDNI. We'd run through these fields, fighting through thick forests of plants, towering high above our heads. Green stalks stretching so tall, touching the sky. Then, we'd totter around on Baba's rusty old cycle, you clutching me tightly, kicking up soil, laughter. Letting life spill over. 'Til you let death overrun.

DHANI. *I* let death overrun? Those miracle seeds aren't full of life. They're full of poison. When the worm starts feeding on the plant, the plant spits out a poison to pierce the worm's intestine. To kill the worm. If those seeds are meant to wipe out the worm, why are the worms getting stronger on Baba's land? Making a meal of his fields?

CHANDNI. If you'd been out here helping him, maybe you could tell me.

DHANI. He didn't do enough.

CHANDNI. He tried. I tried. You repay him with accusations. You repay me by stealing my wages and my dead mother's gold.

DHANI. What?

CHANDNI. I want it all back.

DHANI. I didn't take anything.

CHANDNI. The crop is dead! The harvest is dead! This land is dead! That's all I have of her!

DHANI. I wouldn't do that to you. Or to her.

CHANDNI. I can't listen to your lies anymore!

(**CHANDNI** *turns away from* **DHANI**.)

DHANI. OK. I took the money. But I swear I didn't take the gold.

CHANDNI. *(Shakes him.)* Tell me where you put it. Or who you sold it to? Was it Dev? Rupesh? Jagdeesh? *(Screams.)* Who?

DHANI. *(Holds his head.)* I don't remember taking it! ... Ohhhh, maybe I took it... I don't know... I don't remember...

CHANDNI. Too drunk to live. Too drunk to remember. Too drunk to care. Too drunk, too drunk, too drunk... Like these worms, you sit here sucking the rest of us dry. What about your duty, your responsibility to her, to our father, to me?

DHANI. Duty? Responsibility? Where are you now Chandni?

CHANDNI. You talk about your dreams. I sacrificed my dreams too dear brother.

DHANI. Your choice dutiful daughter.

CHANDNI. Yes, my choice. Which is why I've chosen to go to Amrika with Suraj.

>(**BABA** *falls to his knees on the soil.*)

DHANI. *(Laughs.)* What?

CHANDNI. I'm going to Amrika with Suraj.

DHANI. Achaa? What about your beloved Baba?

CHANDNI. Once we're settled, we can help him from there.

DHANI. You? In my Amrika?

CHANDNI. We talked it through. I saw Suraj last night.

DHANI. I know. You saw him first thing this morning too. Sprawled on your back, skin deep in the fields. Whole village is talking about it Madame Chandni.

>(**CHANDNI** *pushes* **DHANI** *away. Long pause. A car pulls up on the edge of the fields. Car doors slam shut.*)

LAL. *(Offstage.)* Baba Singh! Ohhhh Baba Singh!

>(**LAL** *hurries into the fields, waving a leather folder in the air.* **SURAJ** *follows behind.* **BABA** *slowly comes forward.*)

(Breathless.) Here you are! You didn't get my message?

>(**BABA** *looks distracted.*)

(To **BABA.***)* You were supposed to be at my office four p.m. sharp. Baba, I can't sit around all day watching time pass like you.

SURAJ. Nice job Dhani.

LAL. *(To* **SURAJ.***)* You told *him*?

DHANI. *(Scratching his head.)* I thought I... I... *(Searches down his kurtha and pyjama.)*

LAL. *(To* **SURAJ**.*)* Still much to learn putthar.

> *(***LAL*** moves around inspecting the crops and recoils.* ***CHANDNI*** *runs to* ***SURAJ***.*)*

SURAJ. I thought you'd still be at the school –

CHANDNI. Suraj, our crop is ruined!

SURAJ. *(Looks around.)* I'm... sorry.

CHANDNI. We'll have to talk to Baba later.

> *(***SURAJ*** *nods.* ***BABA*** *moves towards* ***LAL***. ***SURAJ*** *stands back.)*

BABA. Lalji, I've raised this crop like I've raised my own children –

LAL. We all know how that turned out.

BABA. I've lost it all. But with God above, earth below, I'll pay off my debt, somehow.

LAL. I was hoping for a heap of cotton –

DHANI. Not leafy lace, full of holes?

LAL. But we can take it as it is.

CHANDNI. Take what?

LAL. The debt your father owes me.

CHANDNI. He has nothing to pay you with.

LAL. He does.

> *(***CHANDNI*** *looks bemused.)*

You're standing on it.

BABA. *(Shakes his head.)* No...

LAL. *(Opening his folder.)* We just need to sign off a couple of documents.

CHANDNI. *(To* **SURAJ.***)* What's your father doing?

SURAJ. Claiming what he's owed.

CHANDNI. *(Looking around.)* Now?

LAL. Is there a better time?

CHANDNI. *(With folded hands.)* This isn't the time.

LAL. We're on the brink of clinching a huge contract with Dhanwant and The Company in Punjab. Baba, who would have thought? From skinning hides to bona fide businessman. I'm sorry, I need to call in all my debts – immediately.

CHANDNI. *(To* **LAL.***)* How much does Baba owe you?

BABA. *(To* **LAL.***)* That's between you and me.

LAL. According to my figures – three hundred thousand rupees.

BABA. That can't be right.

CHANDNI. Three lakh?

DHANI. *(To* **CHANDNI.***)* So close to Baba and you didn't know?

BABA. It can't be. How is it that much?

LAL. I told you to be careful.

CHANDNI. Baba wouldn't have borrowed that much. It's not possible. Not possible. I want to see those figures!

DHANI. *(Counting his fingers and toes.)* How many flights to Amrika would that have bought me?

*(***LAL*** hands ***CHANDNI*** a sheet of paper.)*

LAL. Only yesterday, your father borrowed six thousand rupees, plus interest.

BABA. I – I borrowed three thousand!

LAL. Here's the rest. *(Holds out more documents for* **CHANDNI** *to read.)* I think you'll find the figures are all in order. Big loans, over several years, plus interest, equal a big debt. Simple maths even a teacher like you understands... Everything on loan, nothing of Baba's own –

CHANDNI. You can't charge interest like this!

LAL. I can. I do.

DHANI. *(To* **BABA.***)* No more loans for you. Your debts have been growing as fat as these worms by the day.

CHANDNI. You can't do this! There must be a law to stop you doing this!

LAL. Not when I have a sale deed, signed by Baba, right here.

> *(***LAL** *pulls a sale deed from the folder.* **CHANDNI** *takes the deed and reads it.)*

BABA. Lalji... we didn't have one...

LAL. *(To* **BABA.***)* Shhh! Hear that sound? The threads are snapping. The wheel is turning...

> *(***BABA** *squats on the soil.)*

BABA. When the land can't breathe, worms don't die. Men do.

CHANDNI. *(Holding the deed, to* **SURAJ.***)* But the land is worth much more than the debt!

SURAJ. *(To* **CHANDNI.***)* It's written in the deed. If Uncle defaults on repaying the loan, he defaults the land.

CHANDNI. All his land? Baba wouldn't have agreed to that! *(Drops before* **BABA.***)* Baba, did you sign this? *(Shakes* **BABA.***)* Baba? Baba, talk to me!

> *(***BABA** *shakes his head from side to side.)*

He didn't sign this! He couldn't have!

LAL. *(Snatches back the deed and holds it aloft.)* His signature – right here.

CHANDNI. A thumbprint?

LAL. *(Holds out the deed.)* Study the whorls if you want.

CHANDNI. He would have told me!

LAL. Did he tell you three hundred thousand rupees of everything?

CHANDNI. *(To* **SURAJ.***)* Please do something!

SURAJ. Dad needs to take what he's owed. He needs to close the deal.

CHANDNI. You can't let him do this!

DHANI. *(To* **BABA.***)* Expensive business losing the farmer's touch.

SURAJ. Uncle would have to pay sooner or later. It would take him years to pay off the whole debt – *(Looking around.)* especially after another bad harvest.

CHANDNI. We'll sell some of our land to pay it off.

LAL. No longer yours to sell.

CHANDNI. If you take all our land, we'll have nothing.

SURAJ. Chandni –

LAL. Chup Suraj.

> *(***SURAJ*** falls silent. ***LAL*** hands ***BABA*** some documents.)*

CHANDNI. What will we eat? What will we do? Where will we go?

LAL. *(To* **BABA.***)* Your signature, to complete the transfer of land.

> *(***LAL*** flips open the inkpad for ***BABA.***)*

CHANDNI. You're torching my father alive!

DHANI. On a cotton stick pyre!

LAL. *(Taps the document.)* Sign on the dotted line.

CHANDNI. Please Lalji. My hands are folded. Give us more time.

LAL. By saving the past, to dispossess the future?

> (**LAL** *directs* **BABA** *to give his thumbprint.* **CHANDNI** *kneels in front of* **BABA**.)

CHANDNI. Baba, don't sign. We'll work something out.

LAL. Like what? He has nothing else. Even with your good looks Chandni, you can't produce three hundred thousand rupees by nightfall.

CHANDNI. *(Getting up.)* I'll go to the police. Or local officials. Tell them about your hideous business. Your illegal dealings.

LAL. What will they do? All this land, all this investment – how do you think they're busying themselves? *(Kneels to the soil, to* **BABA**.*)* Thumbprint here.

DHANI. Like a house of gambling cards, our land is falling down.

CHANDNI. *(Runs over to* **SURAJ** *and takes his hands.)* I beg you. Please.

LAL. Suraj...

SURAJ. We need the land for our business – for our future.

CHANDNI. What about *our* future?

> (**SURAJ** *holds* **CHANDNI**'s *gaze. Pause.* **BABA** *stares vacantly ahead.* **LAL** *steers* **BABA** *to give his thumbprint.*)

LAL. And... here.

CHANDNI. *(To* **LAL** *and* **SURAJ.***)* How can you do this?

> (**LAL** *scans the signatures and blows the ink dry.*)

LAL. Just doing my job. Sorry your father forgot how to do his.

> (**BABA** *rises slowly. As he walks, he stumbles to the ground.* **CHANDNI** *rushes to help. As she holds back tears, he waves her away and walks into the fields.*)

Baba, your land is in clever business hands. When The Company starts reviving this dead land and building the pipeline, they'll need labourers. I'll put in a good word.

DHANI. Lalji, will you hire me?

> (**LAL** *looks* **DHANI** *up and down, before spotting the Neem Tree.*)

LAL. The Neem medicine Tree thrown in too? The Company won't let it go to waste. *(To* **SURAJ.***)* Come on putthar.

SURAJ. Dad, can I –?

LAL. Be quick.

> (**LAL** *begins walking off and* **DHANI** *follows him.*)

DHANI. Lal, Harpurwala village has so much debt, it's put itself up for sale! For sale! A whole village for sale!

LAL. Is that so?

DHANI. Why don't you snap it up? Appoint me head sarpanch?

LAL. *(Pinches* **DHANI***'s cheek.)* Very good! Very good!

(**LAL** *walks off as* **DHANI** *scurries behind him.* **SURAJ** *walks to* **CHANDNI** *and tries to touch her. She pushes him away.*)

SURAJ. Let me explain.

CHANDNI. Like you did last night?

SURAJ. You made a decision like this, not so long ago.

CHANDNI. We've lost everything. You've taken everything.

SURAJ. We'll find Uncle – and Dhani – work for The Company. You have my word.

CHANDNI. We want nothing from you.

SURAJ. It's the only way I can get back there. Please, understand –

CHANDNI. Understand? You stole my honour, stole our land –

SURAJ. I didn't have a choice!

CHANDNI. Did you have a choice when you took me last night? (*Pulls at her clothes and the cotton plants.*) Left me like a corpse, lying in the dirt?

SURAJ. It wasn't like that –

CHANDNI. Grinding me deeper, deeper. My honour to ashes. Soiled. Worthless.

(**SURAJ** *tries to restrain her.* **CHANDNI** *pushes* **SURAJ** *to the ground.*)

Get away from me!

SURAJ. Seeing you again –

CHANDNI. All those years, thinking you'd honour your word. Labh Singh, you're nothing but a black-hearted vulture, feeding on dead flesh!

(**SURAJ** *stares longingly at* **CHANDNI**. **LAL** *runs on with* **DHANI** *in tow, as* **SURAJ** *scrambles up from the ground.*)

LAL. Suraj! Chhaya will be waiting!

(**SURAJ** *closes his eyes.*)

CHANDNI. Chhaya?

LAL. More happy news! Suraj and Chhaya are to be married! Bringing together the two wealthiest, most blessed families, in these villages.

DHANI. Amrikan rascal. Ahhhh, so that's who this is for?

(**DHANI** *pats his pocket and pulls out the necklace. He twirls it in the air.*)

SURAJ. Dhani!

CHANDNI. *(To* **DHANI**.*)* You did take it...

DHANI. *(Points to* **SURAJ**.*)* No. I got it from him.

CHANDNI. My gold? Why did you have my gold?

SURAJ. *Your* gold?

LAL. Not anymore Chandni. Your father gave it to me as a repayment.

CHANDNI. It's not his to give. Not yours to take.

LAL. Ours now, to do as we like. Chhaya will wear it well. *(Holds out his hand.)* Dhani –

(**DHANI** *walks to* **CHANDNI** *and hands her the necklace. She holds it.*)

(To **SURAJ**, *pointing to the necklace.)* We're late.

(**SURAJ** *walks to* **CHANDNI** *and holds her gaze. Pause.*)

Suraj?

(SURAJ *holds out his hand. Pause.* CHANDNI *drops the necklace to the ground.* SURAJ *stoops to pick up the necklace.* SURAJ *takes a final look at* CHANDNI, *before holding out the necklace to* LAL, *who pockets it.* SURAJ *rushes off and* LAL *follows.* CHANDNI *drops to the soil, struggling to hold back tears.*)

DHANI. We might have been wealthy Jats once. But did you really think Lal would let Suraj marry into our pauper family? I see how Chhaya fits the dollar bill.

CHANDNI. What kind of men are you?

DHANI. Accept it Chandni. You're stuck here. Wasting away like the rest of us. Like the peasants we are. Accept your fate. Isn't that what they all say?

(*Long pause.* CHANDNI *rises.*)

CHANDNI. You might have. I won't.

(CHANDNI *rushes off, wiping tears.*)

DHANI. Chandni? Chandni? Where are you going? Chandni? Chandni? The worms! Please don't leave me here with the worms!

(DHANI *runs after* CHANDNI. BABA *slowly walks back to the Neem Tree, dripping in sunset red, his gaze fixed in the distance. He unwinds his turban and ties the cotton cloth to the Neem Tree, looping it around his neck. A slow dhol beat starts up as the cotton fields darken to the Punjabi folk song (or recited poem)* ["PAGRI SAMBHAL JATTA"]* .)

(*Lights out.*)

---

* Licensees are to use the version of Pagri Sambhal Jatta in the public domain

EPILOGUE

KISAAN

In a basanti chunni and shalwar kameez, farmer Chandni Kaur sits cross-legged in the makeshift, draped sleeping quarters of her tractor trolley, decked with kisaan flags. She talks to an unseen, unheard interviewer, on camera. A 'No Farmers, No Food' placard, is visible. [The interview monologue is in video form and can be broken into fragments, with fade-outs and fade-ins between sections.]

My name is Chandni Kaur. I'm a kisaan. A farmer. A daughter of farmers. A daughter of Punjab. One hot, humid evening over a decade ago, I went to check on my father in his fields. I had left him alone there...[*wipes tears.*] I took him roti....brushed hanging spikes of cotton...worm-eaten cotton...looked for him...called out...[*wipes tears.*] The rotis fell...red achaar smeared the stalks...A strong, proud man, head hung low, like the shrivelled crops beneath him...His turban tied from the Neem Tree... cotton folds tight around his neck. Strangled by debt and land-grabbing theft. My heart cracked...like the earth below my teetering feet.

Our government and big companies spent years saying 'Buy GM seeds! Buy stronger pesticides! Grow your crops, grow your profit!' So we did. Drilled into our pockets. Drilled deeper and deeper wells for less and less groundwater, to quench thirsty crops. Spent all we had. Borrowed all we didn't have. Borrowed more. Costs soaring. Interest rates soaring. Our crops failing. A few borrowed rupees became hundreds of thousands of rupees. Debt dragged down my father, 'til he had nowhere to go, except the soil...I held him there, until dawn. Alone. In that field, blackened by ashes. The courts refused to help. Like our ancestral land, we lost our ancestral home. I worked several jobs at once – teacher, labourer, domestic help...took years to pay back debts, determined to buy even half an acre to continue doing the work my father no longer could. Now, I'm a farmer. Like him.

As farmers, we pray for abundance. But we always live on the edge of loss. Every day, I rise at three a.m. to pray, cook, clean, feed and milk the buffalo, save and sow the seeds, till and toil the land, raise the crops as if my children – as my parents taught me. I'm still paying off debts. Only now, I know the real price we're all paying. Our land like desert, our soil poisoned, water poisoned, bodies poisoned, more villagers seriously ill, more farmers taking their lives, by electrocution, drinking pesticides, hanging...

As the killer virus raged and our corona dead burned, our government snuck in three 'anti-farmer' laws. They didn't ask us. Didn't protect us. We're not business people. We're farmers. We serve and feed others. They just slipped the keys to our land to their corrupt billionaire friends. Tied one noose around our fields. Another noose around our necks. Threw us to big markets and big companies, our blood their profit, forcing us into crippling debt – and death. If they sell us off today, they will sell you off tomorrow, until they've got our whole world locked down to profit them and their greedy friends. Bas. Enough.

Tilling my field, I heard those first tractors roar to the Delhi protest camps, demanding the government take back their laws. In the villages, more of us got on our tractors, driving in huge convoys, loaded with village donations and supplies, kisaan flags flying high. Others walked hundreds of miles or cycled, drove in trucks, bringing more sacks of food, blankets, tents, gas cylinders, generators, more things we needed, more things we didn't know we needed – enough to last us months, or years.

In the camp, I sleep in this trolley tractor. Others sleep in tents, some under tarpaulin or cloth, some on the ground, just a blanket between them and this hard country. A neighbouring farmer looks after my land when I'm here. Every few weeks, we swap places. We're all on a rotation system like our crops! If one farmer leaves, ten more come. Our numbers rise.

We've made our own little pind here. With huge langar kitchens to feed everyone, even the police who beat us, or journalists who call us criminals and terrorists. We've got clinics, ambulances, libraries, our own newspapers, including 'Karti Dharti', for the thousands of women protesting. Even roti-rolling machines – and foot massage tents, for our elders! We sleep late, wake before dawn, bathing by the roadside as sisters hold up chaddars, sing Punjabi boliyan, siyappa and kirtan, recite freedom fighting poems, read pamphlets, listen to protest music from Punjabi singers the world over, give speeches so our tone-deaf leaders might hear our pleas.

Instead, our government has tried to force us from our camps. Cut off our words and water, electricity and phones, unleashed goons to attack us, tried to stop more farmers joining us, put up cement barriers and barbed wire, slammed us with tear-gas and icy water canons in icy winter, beaten and arrested us – most shamefully, our elders who fought wars and fed this country, jailing them, jailing brave journalists and fearless daughters like Nodeep Kaur and Disha Ravi. Hundreds have died at their hands, of hypothermia and heart-attacks, in road accidents, self-immolation... Around fires of defiance, we pour energies from growing crops to growing our Chardi Kala spirit – a spirit they can never crush – or sell.

We've organised nationwide labour strikes involving 250 million workers. From hunger strikes and rail rokos to Punjab Bandh and Bharat Bandh, protests continue in villages for those who can't join us at the border, many organised by and involving our women. We might survive corona. But we will not survive these laws. In our growing thousands here, we'll sit through harsh winters, scorching summers, blood-stained cotton and bruises, 'til they hear us. Cheta karo, we're farmers, patient by nature.

We plant seeds one season, look on as bad weather or chemicals destroy our crops another cruel season. Then we sow again, until one season, our harvest finally comes. If the government digs trenches for us to fall through or throws sharp metal spikes in our path, we'll cover them with soil – and grow flowers. We'll grow a real Green Revolution, hands steeped, feet pressed, into the soil. We'll spread roots from these camps into the world, so people will see us and hear us, even as those more powerful try to silence us. I was born on this soil – I'm ready to fight for it. To die for it.

Only this time, I'm not alone.

Kisan Ekta Zindabad!
Kisan Ekta Zindabad!

(Blackout.)

GLOSSARY

PUKKA HOUSE: a solid brick and cement house
MANJA: charpoy
PETI: bridal tin trunk
JHARU: small handheld broom
CHUNNI: a long scarf worn by women over the head and shoulders, usually with a matching shalwar kameez outfit
PAKHI: handheld fan
NEEM TREE: tree native to Punjab and especially, Bathinda
BRUUUUHAAAA!: a traditional farmer's sound to call the goats. Also a jubilant vocal sound used in bhangra or Punjabi folk songs or dances
BHANGRA: traditional folk dance of Punjab, which originated to celebrate the harvest
TURBAN: head covering worn by Sikhs to cover their uncut hair ('kesh' – one of the 5 Ks of Sikhism)
KURTHA: loose-fitting, collarless Indian shirt or top, usually paired with a pyjama
CHAPPALS: pair of Indian slippers or sandals
SHALWAR KAMEEZ: traditional women's dress consisting of a pair of loose, light, ankle-cuffed shalwar trousers and a long kameez tunic top
JUTTIS: traditional gold and silver embroidered, leather slip-on shoes
JALEBIS: sticky bright orange Indian sweets made of swirls of deep-fried batter, dipped in sugary syrup
KARA: a symbolic Sikh steel or iron bangle, one of the Sikh 5 Ks
GLASSY: glass of whisky
SIKH: a follower of Sikhism
BHETI: affectionate term for a daughter
GIDDHA: women's traditional folk/harvest dance in Punjab, energetically performed in circles, to rhythmic clapping and boliyan (traditional folk songs)
JAT: an agricultural caste of farmers and peasants, especially from Punjab
HEER: the smart, feisty, beautiful village girl from 'Heer Ranjha', one of Punjab's most famous tragic romances about star-crossed lovers
SHAAVASH: well done, bravo
ROTI: chappati or flat round bread cooked on a tava (griddle pan)
DAL: a staple Punjabi lentil dish
SAAG: a staple Punjabi dish containing spinach or other leafy greens
SABJI: a staple Punjabi dish made of any type of vegetable or combination of vegetables
JALANDHAR: an ancient city in the Doaba region of Punjab with a history of migration abroad, both legal and illegal
ACHAA: various meanings, depending on usage – 'oh really', 'ok', 'right', 'good', 'I see/understand', 'so'
RABBA: God

GAL SUN: listen to me
GT ROAD: one of the longest and most historic roads in South Asia, the Grand Trunk Road runs from Afghanistan through India and Pakistan to Bangladesh
AMRIKAN: Punjabi pronunciation for American
CHARDI KALA: a Punjabi expression of optimism/living in a positive spiritual state of mind; roughly translated as 'Keep spirits high!'
VAISAKHI: One of two major seasonal harvests in Punjab. Vaisakhi is the annual spring harvest and is marked by a huge festival on 13th or 14th April, which also marks the beginning of the Punjabi New Year. Vaisakhi also celebrates the founding of the Khalsa Panth, the Sikh Community, on 13 April 1699.
FITTEH MOO: an expression of annoyance or exasperation, akin to a face-palm
BEWAKOOF: stupid or foolish person
KALA BHOOT: Evil spirit
KALJUG: an age of darkness and ignorance in humanity's spiritual cycle
RUPEE: Indian currency
BADMAASH: a bad, dishonest, rogue person or troublemaker
BHANG: marijuana
AFEEM: raw opium
BHUKKI: poppy husk opioid
BIBI: a respectful term for a woman, usually an older one
HAIN: what?
HAAH: yes
AMRIKA: a Punjabi village ideal of America
PAISE-PINCHING: penny-pinching; 'paise' is Indian currency (100 paise = 1 rupee)
BALLE BALLE: an expression of happiness or excitement when bhangra dancing, partying or having a good time
CHUP KAAR!: shut up!/be quiet!
NAY: no
PAKORA: deep-fried batter Punjabi snack, usually containing vegetables
BHARAT MATA: India personified as a Mother Goddess – Mother India
GREEN REVOLUTION: the American-influenced Green Revolution aimed to feed India's millions and was introduced in the fertile region of Punjab in the 1960s/1970s. Traditional farming methods, techniques and equipment were replaced with modern Western ones e.g. hybrid seeds (artificially produced seeds), chemicals (pesticides, herbicides, fungicides and fertilisers), machines (tractors, tubewells and threshers) and intensive irrigation. Initially, the Green Revolution was a huge success, producing high yields and profits that helped earn Punjab the nickname 'breadbasket of India'.
GENE REVOLUTION: sometimes called a 'Second Green Revolution', the Gene Revolution is based on the use of biotechnology (science and

technology) to increase crop yields e.g. genetically modified (GM) seeds and chemicals to make GM seeds grow
ZAMEEN: land
PUTH/PUTTHAR: affectionate term for a beloved son
CHARKHA: a spinning wheel, especially for cotton
GREAT DIVIDE: Partition (referring to the August 1947 Partition of British India into the two independent nations of India and Pakistan – and the state of Punjab into Indian Punjab and Pakistani Punjab)
SAT SRI AKAL: Sikh greeting in Punjabi, roughly translated as 'True is the Timeless One'.
CHULHA: a small, traditional earthen or brick cooking stove
PHULKARI: traditional Punjabi floral-patterned, hand-embroidery
TRINJAN: when village girls and women traditionally came together in a spirit of creativity and community to spin charkhas, weave, knit, cook, eat, talk, gossip, sing folk songs, giddha dance, exchange advice and wisdom and learn together
BESHARAM: shameless
AAJA: come/come here
KIDDHA?: how are you?
THEEK: fine/OK
BAS: enough
BAKWAAS: rubbish/nonsense
WAH JI WAH: wow; so great; expression of awe or happy surprise
BARFI: dense milk-based coloured Indian sweets, flavoured with fruit, nuts, spices
KOTHI: big Punjabi house or mansion
YAAR: friend
KI PATHA: who knows?
BAK BAK: yap yap/nonsense chat
CHAA: tea
PHOREN: foreign
DAKU: bandit/robber
EK MINUTE: one minute
CROREPATI: millionaire
BAPU: father
KABADDI: ancient Indian contact sport, popular in Punjab, involving two teams of seven on a circular court (often sand), who try to raid each other's half, while tagging the opposite team. Kabaddi combines wrestling, tag and continuous chants of 'kabaddi' while holding one's breath
WWF: World Wrestling Federation
LUCHA LAFANGHA: a good for nothing vagabond
SONIYE: pretty girl or woman/beautiful one
BHATURA: deep-fried soft and puffy bread, traditionally eaten with chole or channa (chickpeas)

PARANTHAS: a tava (griddle pan)–fried traditional flat bread, cooked plain or stuffed with various mixed vegetable or occasionally, meat fillings
ACHAAR: pickle
ZAMINDAR: a (wealthy) landowner
RAKHRI: 'Rakhri' means 'to protect'. An August festival to celebrate the bond between brothers and sisters. The festival involves the sister tying a rakhri thread on her brother and praying for his well-being in return for a vow of brotherly protection and gifts
DESI: native to India/Punjab/one's home 'desh' country; homegrown
SARPANCH: head of a village
DHOL: double-sided barrel drum, traditionally used in Punjabi folk and bhangra music

EPILOGUE GLOSSARY
BASANTI: spring/colour yellow; also, the colour (with green) of the protesting farmers
CHUNNI: a long scarf worn by women over the head and shoulders, usually with a matching shalwar kameez outfit
SHALWAR KAMEEZ: traditional women's dress consisting of a pair of loose, light, ankle-cuffed shalwar trousers and a long kameez tunic top
KISAAN: farm worker - farmers or labourers
ROTI: chappati or flat round bread cooked on a tava (griddle pan)
ACHAAR: pickle
BAS: enough
PIND: village
LANGAR: volunteer run Sikh community kitchens, serving free vegetarian meals to all
CHADDAR: long piece of cloth or sheet
BOLIYAN: emotive Punjabi couplets, often sung to accompany bhangra or giddha dances
SIYAPPA: mourning songs
KIRTAN: Sikh devotional songs or music, especially sacred hymns and shabads (verses) from the Guru Granth Sahib, the Sikh holy book
CHARDI KALA: a Punjabi expression of optimism/living in a positive spiritual state of mind; roughly translated as 'Keep spirits high!'
ROKO: march or protest involving blocking a railway or road
BANDH: strike/shutdown
CHETA KARO: remember
KISAN EKTA ZINDABAD: Long Live Farmer-Labourer Unity

www.ingramcontent.com/pod-product-compliance
Ingram Content Group UK Ltd.
Pitfield, Milton Keynes, MK11 3LW, UK
UKHW021907060225
454771UK00026B/484